The
Other Side
——— of ———
Software

SECOND EDITION

The
Other Side
of
Software

A USER'S GUIDE
FOR DEFINING
SOFTWARE REQUIREMENTS

SECOND EDITION

Carolyn Shamlin

amacom
American Management Association

This book is available at a special
discount when ordered in bulk quantities.
For information, contact Special Sales Department,
AMACOM, a division of American Management Association,
135 West 50th Street, New York, NY 10020.

Library of Congress Cataloging-in-Publication Data

Shamlin, Carolyn.
    The other side of software : a user's guide for defining software
requirements / Carolyn Shamlin. -- 2nd ed., 1st AMACOM pbk. ed.
        p.   cm.
    Rev. ed. of: A user's guide for defining software requirements.
c1985.
    Includes bibliographical references.
    ISBN 0-8144-7739-9
    1. Computer software--Development.   I. Shamlin, Carolyn.   User's
guide for defining software requirements. II. Title.
[QA76.76.D47S48   1990]
005.36--dc20   89-48313
                                                            CIP

First AMACOM paperback edition, 1990.
Originally published as *A User's Guide for Defining Software Requirements*
by QED Information Sciences, Inc.

Printing number

10 9 8 7 6 5 4 3 2 1

To Don

who offered both occasion and encouragement for writing this book, my gratitude for his unselfish input and support.

CONTENTS

List of Figures   **xi**
Foreword   **xiii**
Preface   **xv**
Preface to the First Edition   **xvii**

PART 1:
How to Use Your Expertise to Maximum Advantage   **1**

Chapter 1:
The User's Role in Systems Development   **3**
Separating the Problem Definition from the Problem Solution   3
The Benefits of User-developed Specifications   4
A Systems Development Overview   7

Chapter 2:
The Starting Point   **9**
Assessment of Needs   9
Establishment of System Goals and Objectives   12
Defining the Scope of the System   15
Keeping the System Simple   16
Cost-benefit Tradeoffs   19

Chapter 3:
Define the System in Data Terms   **25**
The Input-Process-Output Model   25
The External System   27
The Interface System   29
The Internal System   37
A Summary of System Inputs and Outputs   38
Analysis Questions to Be Answered   39

PART 2:
How to Develop System Specifications   **43**

Chapter 4:

Find Structures that Simplify **45**

A Top-down Approach to Systems Analysis 45

An Overview of an Analysis Plan 53

Chapter 5:

Ten Steps to a Requirements Definition **61**

Define Information Needs 61

Determine Required Inputs 63

Define Data Relationships 66

Define Computer Outputs 67

Define Inquiry Capabilities 69

Identify Sources of Inputs 70

Define Data-Entry Procedures 72

Specify Data Validation Procedures 75

Define Data Protection Requirements 75

Specify Data Derivation Rules 78

Chapter 6:

The Continuing Role of the User **81**

Computer Design Review 81

External Procedure Design 82

Acceptance Testing 83

System Evaluation 85

PART 3:

How to Control the End Results **87**

Chapter 7:

Management Strategies **89**

Organizational Structures and Their Effects 89

Measuring Progress During Software Development 91

Chapter 8:

Support for a Usable System **101**

Integrated Documentation 101

Integrated User Training 104

Human-Friendly Interfaces 108

Chapter 9:

Planning for Change **115**

Changes in Functional Requirements 115

Changes in Data Requirements 119

Application Integration and Evolution 122

Contents

PART 4:
How to Increase Management Productivity Through Computers   **129**

Chapter 10:
Target Areas for End-user Computing   **131**
   Trends in Technology   131
   Improving Communications Through Office Automation Systems   132
   Improving Planning Through Decision Support Systems   132
   Improving Tracking and Control Through Executive Information
   Systems   134

Chapter 11:
Factors Promoting Successful Executive Information Systems   **139**
   Support Requirements   139
   An "Executive Champion"   140
     An "Operating Sponsor"   141
     Technical Staffing   141
   Technology Issues   142
     Should an EIS be mainframe- or micro-based, or operate within a
       cooperative processing environment?   142
     What software capabilities are needed to build an EIS?   144
     Should an EIS have its own data base or should it have direct access
       to the corporate operational data bases?   145
   Data Feeder Systems   146
   The Politics of EIS   147

Chapter 12:
Design of Executive Information Systems Applications   **149**
   Functional Requirements   149
     Minimal Training   149
     Navigation Paths   149
     Information Compression   151
   Prototyping as a Design and Development Methodology   157
   Data Requirements   163
   Focus on Business Objectives and Problems   166
   System Expansion   168

Summary   **171**
Bibliography   **175**
Index   **177**

LIST OF FIGURES

Chapter 2
Figure 1: Software package evaluation   21
Chapter 3
Figure 2: System levels   26
Figure 3: System data flow   27
Figure 4: External system data flow   30
Figure 5: Input-process-output model   38
Chapter 4
Figure 6: A top-down approach   47
Figure 7: A top-down budget development structure   48
Figure 8: A top-down structure for a party menu   50
Figure 9: Two structures for a menu plan   51
Figure 10: A top-down structure for a sales management
     system   54
Figure 11: Subsystems of a sales management system   55
Figure 12: Outline of a requirements definition   58
Chapter 5
Figure 13: External system model   61
Figure 14: A top-down structure for analyzing information
     needs   62
Figure 15: A top-down structure for analyzing required inputs   64
Figure 16: Grouping data items by keys   68
Figure 17: Interface system model   69
Figure 18: Sample input transactions   71
Figure 19: Transaction specifications   72
Figure 20: Internal system model   74
Figure 21: Data protection requirements   77
Chapter 7
Figure 22: Sample system to produce a financial statement   99
Figure 23: Comparisons of top-down approaches   99

Chapter 8
Figure 24: Prompts for a payroll system   109
Figure 25: Menus for a sales management system   110
Figure 26: Skeletal-screen data entry   113
Chapter 9
Figure 27: Applications and subject data bases used   125
Figure 28: Application levels, users, and methods   127
Chapter 10
Figure 29: Differences between decision support systems
     and EIS   135
Figure 30: Management and technology influences on success
     factors   140
Figure 31: EIS functional requirements   152
Figure 32: Sample top menu   153
Figure 33: Sample second menu   155
Figure 34: Sample third menu   156
Figure 35: Sample exception menu   158
Figure 36: Differences in needs of executives and operational
     managers   159
Figure 37: Selection of EIS application areas   167

FOREWORD

Altogether too many software systems are created with only the sketchiest understanding of how the system is to be used and what its business purposes are. This is especially true for systems that are designed to provide information to *knowledge workers*. The usefulness of an information system depends not only on whether the answers can be obtained, but on how much time and effort it takes to get the answer. Not only must the end result be relevant to the user, but the end result must be obtainable with an effort level that is commensurate with the value of the information received.

Part of the job of information systems professionals is to learn to communicate with end users and understand their problems. It is a creative give-and-take process. In this book, Carolyn Shamlin explains why end users have to be involved in the process of defining software requirements and why their involvment is an ongoing process, not simply an upfront exercise.

One of the most striking developments in the technology of information retrieval has been Executive Information Systems (EIS). This latest edition of *Defining Software Requirements* includes a new chapter on EIS which is based on Ms. Shamlin's experience as an executive with one of the leading vendors in the field.

Executives are a demanding group of users who are becoming increasingly involved in the application of computers as strategic weapons. They have learned that business competes globally, and that systems must become part of a global strategy. It has been said many times that managers make decisions based on incomplete information. This must change and this book provides the guidance for working with users at all levels to develop systems for the future. It should prove valuable to any IS professional who has responsibility for delivering applications and solutions. The concepts are funda-

mental to getting your money's worth from IS projects and the principles explained herein, if applied competently, will produce greatly
improved effectivenss of development efforts.

David Friend
Chairman
Pilot Executive Software

PREFACE

Since the first edition of this book, computers have indeed come out of the information systems back offices and basements. Personal computers have proliferated at all levels in organizations: secretaries use word processors, professionals use spreadsheets, managers use project scheduling systems, and everyone uses electronic mail. Significant technology advances have put powerful computing in the hands of anyone with a few thousand dollars to spend. Where hardware costs and programmer-oriented software once presented substantial barriers to independent computer use, newer-generation software and hardware extend computing power to everyone.

The massive infiltration of personal computers into organizations paved the way for more user-oriented software tools, particularly in the areas of word processing and data analysis. Advances in micro to mainframe links, usage of departmental minicomputers, and availability of electronic mail systems have all contributed to new ways of using technology to increase productivity. We are now experiencing the advent of new standards for software interfacing that will further facilitate the integration of these varied tools, leading to even greater opportunities for gains in productivity.

This second edition includes a new section on the current status of corporate computing directions and how the end user might take advantage of the technnology. This new section, "How to Increase Management Productivity Through Computers," discusses the current trends in end-user computing, including office automation, decision support, and executive information systems (EIS).

Executive Information Systems are directed toward the highest level of management within a company—those who have traditionally shied away from computers. As the baby boom generation, with its increased background in computers, begins to invade the executive suites of major corporations, computers will play a larger role in the way these executives perform their work, which will in turn have a large impact on the way organizations are run. Some companies are already scratching the surface and discovering that implementing an EIS may indeed modify organizational behavior and the seats of organization power.

PREFACE TO
THE FIRST EDITION

This book is for people with primary professional interests in areas other than computers who want to use computers to advantage within their areas of responsibility and expertise. If you are the manager of a corporate or operational function that might benefit from effective use of computing resources, this book provides a framework for analyzing your requirements and communicating them clearly to software developers.

Computer system users may not want—nor should they be required—to burden themselves with the technical details and jargon of the computer industry in order to communicate their requirements effectively to software producers. To assist in this process, this book offers a concise and practical discussion of a comprehensive set of relevant topics written at the consumer (end-user) level.

Software development tools continue to improve and will become increasingly more accessible to the user directly. Users should be aware, however, that although less actual programming will be involved in developing applications in the future, analyzing and defining the application requirements will continue to be necessary.

This book addresses the following subjects:

Part 1: How to use *your* expertise to maximum advantage

Part 2: How to develop system specifications

Part 3: How to control the end results

The methods presented and the issues discussed will be useful for:

- users who must specify their computer system needs and requirements or justify them to upper management, or do both,

- users who are considering the purchase or development of application software,
- users who want to control the factors determining success of software development projects,
- managers or supervisors of functions that might benefit from effective use of computers,
- executives and others who must make decisions concerning computer software investment and resource allocation.

My experience working with users during the last twenty years has convinced me that the single most important factor determining the success of software projects is active involvement of end-user managers and staff who thoroughly understand their system requirements. This book provides end users with a methodology for conducting their own systems analysis, developing a comprehensive system requirement specification, and controlling the end results.

For the things we have to learn before we can do them, we learn by doing them.

—Aristotle

Part One

HOW TO USE YOUR EXPERTISE TO MAXIMUM ADVANTAGE

We know better the needs of ourselves than of others;
to serve oneself is economy of administration.
—Ambrose Bierce
The Devil's Dictionary

Chapter 1

THE USER'S ROLE IN SYSTEMS DEVELOPMENT

SEPARATING THE PROBLEM DEFINITION FROM THE PROBLEM SOLUTION

Before a product can be efficiently produced, it must first be designed, typically in accordance with some overall design specifications. These specifications derive from the basic goals for the product, that is, its intended function. In addition to functional goals, other goals may be relevant, such as developmental, operational, and maintenance costs; expected benefits and results; quality standards; and optional extra features. The nature of the product will determine the level of detail necessary for the design specification to ensure adequate product development. The levels may range from those dealing with external appearance to the characteristics of internal function. At each level of design, a distinction can be made between the design specification and the actual design itself. The specification describes *what* is required, and the actual design describes *how* the requirement will be met.

When the product is a computer software system, the user is the expert concerning *what* is needed and should communicate these requirements clearly to the software producers (the system designers and programmers), who then apply their computer expertise to *how* to produce a system to meet these requirements.

The design specifications are the foundation on which an application system is built. If these specifications fail to describe clearly *what* is required from the system, luck and accident are unnecessarily permitted to influence the resulting product. The user sacrifices considerable control over the end results, since the producers then have the opportunity to make guesses about what the user meant to say or to devise a system based on their perception of the user's needs.

Inadequate specifications can result from two kinds of errors:

1. Some requirements are simply omitted from the specifications and the specifications are therefore incomplete.
2. The specifications fail to state directly *what* is needed and instead specify the user's idea of a solution.

The effects of the first type of error are obvious, while those of the latter are more subtle. In the second type, the producers are not only unnecessarily constrained from producing the best possible solution, since the user has specified a particular solution as a requirement, but they are left to infer "what is needed" from the "how to provide it." If we assume that the software producers have more computer expertise than the user and, conversely, that the user has more knowledge about the function to be supported by the computer, we realize that an error of this type fails to use available resources to maximum advantage. This error is most easily avoided by treating the design specification as the *problem definition* phase and the system design as the *problem solution* phase.

The user is responsible for the adequacy of the design specification and must ultimately evaluate how well the software meets these requirements. As the user, you should ultimately evaluate the system results in terms of the stated objectives and design specifications: "Did I receive what I ordered?"

THE BENEFITS OF USER-DEVELOPED SPECIFICATIONS

Active involvement of the user through meaningful project reviews during the software development and implementation stages is necessary in order to refine design decisions. Continuing involvement permits corrections to be made at the earliest point, when the least investment has been made in wrong directions. Early error detection and correction will minimize system development costs. Some of the system goals may create design conflicts (for example, the need to minimize costs versus the need to maximize function). So, to retain control over end results, the user must be responsible for assessing the costs and benefits of alternative design proposals and for making the final decisions.

If the user prepares a well-defined set of system objectives and specific requirements, the software producers should be able to present their design proposals in terms that are meaningful and understandable to the user. In fact, the user should insist on design proposal formats and terminology that are directly relatable to the specifications, and should not accept those presented in computer jargon, which confuses more than it clarifies. The chances of receiving a software design proposal presented in understandable terms is greatly increased if it has been prepared in response to a comprehensive set of requirements. *To facilitate communication with the developers, you should avoid the technical jargon of your own profession in your requirements document.*

As the direct user of the system, you are the most knowledgeable person regarding your needs and hence should be the one to define them. You would not have to know the intricacies of home construction to provide an architect with the design specifications for the house you want to build. You would specify your external requirements in terms that are meaningful to you, such as overall size, number and types of rooms, cost, overall style, and the functions that you expect the house to serve. Using this information, the architect would respond with several design alternatives from which you would choose. In those areas in which not all of your criteria could be met simultaneously, you would choose the options that best suited your needs.

In areas where some requirements are omitted from the software design specification, you are dependent on the judgment of the designer. Although such judgment may be competent and even insightful, it is unlikely to be based on direct content knowledge and experience. What you will be offered as design proposals, therefore, will usually be less than what you could have received if you had clearly specified your requirements.

To the extent that your specifications state all of your requirements—that is, comprehensively describe all the relevant aspects of the problem—the more control you retain over the final product. Conversely, going beyond specifying *what* you require, to specifying *how* to incorporate it into the design, will not only overconstrain the designers from fully applying their technical expertise, but will result in a system that may be both more expensive and less satisfactory. Limiting the specifications to the real needs that must be met by the end product, and at what costs, will permit the designers to provide realistic design alternatives from which you, the user, may choose. The alternatives will be far more realistic because the designers understand the external requirements that must be satisfied. The user remains in the role of decision maker and controls the direction of product development.

The user will derive these additional benefits from the effort involved in producing an adequate design specification:

1. an in-depth understanding of the real needs to be met by the system and, therefore, a basis for subsequent decision making and system evaluation;
2. a comprehensive analysis of the relevant external factors, and thus a broader context in which to design and develop supporting computer software;
3. a thorough assessment of needs and an establishment of priorities, goals, and objectives, providing a basis for cost justifications and feasibility proposals for upper management.

Even if you are both end user and software producer, making the distinction between design specifications and the design itself will prove useful. You will avoid overconstraining your own design or never fully understanding the problem to be solved by the system. Often when we are immersed in the details of devising solutions, we risk having our solutions become our problems and we forget the real needs and goals. To avoid the trap of not seeing the forest for the trees, we should keep our goals separate from the steps that must be taken to achieve them. It is essential to communicate *what* the problem is before we begin producing and evaluating solutions. A solution that happens to solve an ill-defined problem is an accident, albeit a fortunate one. If the same resources and efforts were applied to solving a well-defined problem, a better solution would much more likely be found.

As the user, you are probably paying for the development or acquisition of software, either directly or indirectly. You should use your resources most efficiently toward the goal of obtaining a computer system that best serves your needs. You want a system that performs as you expect for a reasonable cost.

A SYSTEMS DEVELOPMENT OVERVIEW

The major tasks required to develop a computer application system can be divided into four phases. Those in italics are the primary responsibility of the user.

Analysis Phase:
1. *Define external system needs.*
2. *Establish system goals and objectives.*
3. *Determine information requirements.*
4. *Specify interface requirements.*
5. *Specify data relationships.*
6. *Specify processing requirements.*
7. *Specify basic and optional features.*

Design Phase:
1. Design computer data base.
2. Design computer programs.
3. Specify computer hardware requirements.
4. Prepare cost estimates.
5. *Review design proposals.*
6. *Analyze costs and benefits.*
7. *Decide among design alternatives.*

Implementation Phase:
1. Develop computer software.
2. Obtain computer equipment.
3. *Train end user staff.*
4. *Obtain necessary supplies, such as forms.*
5. *Develop user-acceptance tests.*

Evaluation Phase:
1. *Conduct user-acceptance test.*
2. *Evaluate test results.*
3. *Specify needed adjustments.*
4. Correct system.

The development of computer software to support an application system should be a cooperative venture between end users and computer staff. Much of the actual work required to accomplish the listed tasks can be shared. End user management, however, should retain the primary responsibility for those tasks so indicated.

The end product of the analysis phase is the design specification. Part 1 of this book presents a framework for understanding which requirements to specify. Part 2 provides a methodology for developing and analyzing the requirements and communicating them to programming staff. Part 3 covers state-of-the-art system development tools and strategies for project management during the design, implementation, and evaluation phases.

Chapter 2

THE STARTING POINT

ASSESSMENT OF NEEDS

Each step in the analysis of user needs will build on the information gathered in the prior steps. Therefore, the initial tasks are critical, and you should allocate sufficient time and resources to ensure that they are done well. The first chapter described the design specification phase as that of problem definition and the design and implementation phases as those of problem solution. Within this framework, and borrowing from general problem-solving and management theory, we can readily develop a list of initial tasks and apply them to systems analysis.

1. Assess the needs of the external system.
2. Based on these needs, set goals for the problem solution.
3. For each goal, establish a set of measurable objectives that, taken together, achieve the goal.

These steps provide the basis for the design specification. By clearly defining the needs and establishing specific goals and objectives, you permit the designers' efforts to be focused on solving a well-defined problem within stated constraints, such as budget, schedule, and the like. As the user, you will also be able to perform the crucial management function of determining progress toward goals and making mid-course corrections when progress is off-track or unsatisfactory. Such a function presumes the existence of goals and measurable objectives.

Whether you are considering using computers in a new area or replacing an old system with a new one, both situations can be viewed as recognizing a need to improve the current system. The types of improvements will depend on the nature of the product or process you manage.

For example, a sales manager may need to achieve certain improvements in a sales management system. The general type of improvement is shown on the left and the specific need of the sales system is on the right.

Type of Improvement	*Specific System Need*
1. Improve quality or accuracy of available data.	Provide more accurate sales forecasts.
2. Increase volume of data processed.	Be able to handle twice the current sales volume.
3. Increase speed at which data is processed.	Process sales orders in half the current time.
4. Decrease costs for processing data.	Process orders at 60 percent of current costs.
5. Enhance capabilities of current functions.	Improve tracking and follow-up of sales leads.
6. Expand responsibilities to include new functions.	Conduct postsales customer surveys and analyze results.

The type of improvement you need will focus attention on current procedures that should be investigated. Using the general categories of improvement in the sales example, the following guideline indicates where to focus attention in analyzing your current system.

Identify Functions in Which:	*To Achieve These Goals:*
errors are introduced,	improvement of quality or accuracy of available data,
time spent is disproportionately high,	increase in volume of data processed,
bottlenecks occur,	increase in speed at which data is processed,
costs are disproportionately high,	decrease in costs,

Identify Functions in Which:	*To Achieve These Goals:*
current procedures fail to satisfy all requirements,	enhancement of capabilities in current areas,
related additional requirements could be met.	expansion of responsibilities to include new functions.

A system has a purpose—some type of work to accomplish or some function to provide in support of other systems. James G. Miller, in *Living Systems*, provides a working definition:

A system is a set of interacting units with relationships among them.

In this book, this system of people, their tools, and their procedures form the external system (external to the computer). All these units must interact in order to accomplish the work of the system, and the external system needs are those that should be defined in the needs assessment. The people involved in getting the work of the system done and the tools, materials, and procedures that they use form a system.

The needs assessment should be as comprehensive as possible. When analyzing your current procedures, identify those needs that are presently being met in addition to those that are not. The statement of needs should not be related to computers or to the current procedures per se; instead, they should be statements of external system needs. The current procedures may include tasks that only indirectly relate to the real goals of the system. For example, they may have been needed when most of the processes were manual, but are inappropriate in an automated system. If you start with defining the real goals and needs of the system, you are less likely to carry over unnecessary tasks to the new environment.

In the sales example, the identified needs are not related to computers but rather to the external system needs. Some requirements may have been externally imposed on the sales manager, such as reducing the costs of processing orders. Other needs may stem from anticipated changes in circumstances, such as being able to handle twice the current sales volume. Still others may derive from the desire to improve managerial capacity, such as providing more accurate sales forecasts.

ESTABLISHMENT OF SYSTEM GOALS AND OBJECTIVES

Once the external system needs are defined, they must be translated into goals for the computer system. Goals should be carefully stated in terms of results to be achieved rather than in terms of ways to achieve them. One goal may address multiple needs, but each need should be satisfied if all the goals are to be met. Develop a mapping of which goals address which needs, since the goals often require adjustment during a later stage. This mapping will permit you to analyze the impact of your decisions on the system needs and provide you with a basis for making well-informed decisions.

To illustrate this process, let us take a look at the sales management needs presented earlier. Examples of proposed system goals are shown below each statement of need.

1. Provide more accurate sales forecasts.
   a. At user request, the system must be able to produce sales forecast figures for various periods, such as a month, a quarter, or a year. These figures should reflect sales trends over the last two years using data from the most recent sales period as a base and adjusting for seasonal variations.
   b. The user should have the option to request this report in either tabular or graphical form.
2. Handle twice the current sales volume.
   a. The current manual system for order processing requires three persons to handle 500 orders per week. The new system must be able to process up to 1,000 orders per week without the need to increase staff allocated to this function.
3. Process sales orders in half the current time.
   a. Currently, four days are required to process an order from initial receipt to the shipping dock. With the new system in place, processing time should not exceed two days.

4. Process orders at 60 percent of current costs.
   a. It currently costs $5.00 in labor and materials to process each order. With the new system, costs should not exceed $3.50 per order, including cost for staff, terminals, and computer time.
5. Improve tracking and follow-up of sales leads.
   a. On request, the system should produce a report of sales leads by city or state, for use in trip planning.
   b. On request, the system should produce a report of sales leads that have not been contacted for a specified period, for use in resource allocation.
6. Conduct postsales customer surveys and analyze results.
   a. When a customer's order includes a product not ordered before, the system should generate the appropriate customer survey form when the invoice is produced.
   b. The system should be able to analyze the results of these surveys and produce statistical summaries and customer profiles.

The next stage of the process is establishing measurable objectives for each goal. The objectives may be smaller in scope than the goals, but should remain results-oriented. Since a goal may cut across many dimensions, you may find it necessary to establish a goal for each dimension. For example, if a goal is to increase the profit margin, a separate objective for each component may be required, such as decreasing costs by 10 percent and increasing sales by 20 percent. Quantifiable measures are highly desirable since they are easy to assess and subject to the least misinterpretation. Time is well spent in attempting to state all objectives in quantifiable terms. When qualifiable objectives are used, you should define the criteria for the qualitative judgments that will be used to evaluate the system results.

Again using the sales example, measurable objectives for each goal within need 5 above (improve tracking and follow-up of sales leads) are shown below.

1. On request, the system should produce a report of sales leads by city or state, for use in trip planning.
   a. The sales staff who will request and use this report are

not those who normally interact with the computer system; therefore, making this request should be easy (not requiring more than a couple of minutes of instruction).

    b. Since these users are not likely to have a terminal in their offices, they should be able to see the report on a screen within a minute or two and receive a printed copy of it within an hour.

2. On request, the system should produce a report of sales leads that have not been contacted for a specified period, for use in resource allocation.

    a. This report is one of several that will be used by sales management to analyze the effectiveness of sales staff locations and to project travel expenses. Data presented on this report, therefore, must be in a form that permits it to be selectively fed into a modeling system. The spread sheet thus generated will enable management to analyze effective allocation of sales staff by geographic region. The procedures for requesting this data should not require more than a few minutes, and both the model and the report should be produced within twenty minutes of the request.

    b. Sales leads originate from at least three sources: sales receptionist via telephone inquiries, marketing staff via responses to advertisements, and direct entry by sales representatives. The data collection process should accomodate the needs of this diverse group of end users, some of whom will only occasionally use the system while others will use it daily. Evaluation of this objective will be based on required time for end-user training, error rate, and time required to correct errors.

The measurable objectives for each goal should form a set that, if each objective is individually met, will result in the overall goal being met. The methods described in this book permit revisions to these needs, goals, and objectives throughout the design process; however, your initial list should be as comprehensive as possible. If you find a goal that you cannot relate to any of the stated needs, you should take another look at the system—perhaps a need was omitted.

Each goal should relate to a need and each need should be addressed by the goals.

DEFINING THE SCOPE OF THE SYSTEM

In the process of defining the needs, goals, and objectives of the system, you must also determine the scope of the computer system. In most cases, only some of the external functions will involve computer assistance, while other functions will remain completely manual. Which functions should involve the computer will be determined by the nature of the process. This question can be answered by asking: Can the computer be usefully employed in this task, and is the benefit cost-justifiable?

For those functions in which computer support appears useful, the costs and benefits must be analyzed. Two possible approaches are:

1. Assume initially that all of these functions will be automated and then proceed to eliminate those functions for which automation costs are determined to exceed the benefits.
2. Assume that no function will be automated until both costs and benefits are determined and shown to be in a favorable ratio.

For the designers, the problem with the second approach is that the costs associated with each function cannot be determined in isolation. Certain overhead costs are necessarily present whether one or fifty functions are automated. In addition, the benefits to be derived are not always traceable to the automation of a single function, since automating one can increase the benefits to be derived from automating others.

Suppose that we wish to determine the costs of automating sales forecasts in our sales management system. If we assume the automation of order processing, then most of the necessary data will already be available within the computer. Costs for the sales forecast report will be limited to the one-time cost of developing the forecasting program and will not need to include costs for data collection and software to edit and maintain this information. Such costs are already borne by the order entry function. It is more meaningful to assume the automation of the order processing system and then determine the marginal costs of adding a sales forecasting component.

For these reasons, I recommend the following steps to define the scope of the system.

1. Decide on the minimal set of basic functions to automate, restricting this list to those that are known empirically to be amenable to computer processing at reasonable cost.
2. Specify these functions as the basic system for which the designers are to provide cost data.
3. Specify remaining functions as optional extensions to the basic system. Marginal cost data should be requested for each of these functions.
4. Quantify the benefits to be derived from the basic system and from each of the optional functions.

KEEPING THE SYSTEM SIMPLE

The smallest actual good is better than the most magnificent promises of impossibilities.
—Thomas Macauley,
Francis Bacon

Computer software projects often fail because the requirements are ill-defined or grandiose. These particular factors can be controlled by the user by choosing an appropriate set of functions to automate and by carefully defining the requirements. Limit the scope of the initial system to those functions that:

1. have well-defined benefits to be derived from automation;
2. will be used in areas that are already well-organized and understood; (Computers never compensate for poor management.)

Exclude from the system any functions for which:

1. the information needs are not clearly understood;
2. the system objectives cannot be defined in specific, measurable terms;
3. the benefits from automation are abstract and intangible.

After the initial system is installed, other functions can be added as needs become more clearly defined. The last chapter of this book discusses software tools that permit your system to be extended in the future.

Another reason for the failure of software projects is the lack of end-user involvement in the design and development processes. As the person responsible for specifying system requirements, you are likely to have management authority over many of the potential end users. In this context, the end users are those persons who directly interact with the computer system, such as those who prepare data for the computer files, those who use terminals to enter data or request reports, and those who use and interpret outputs produced by the computer. As their manager, or as the responsible management representative, you must ensure that sufficient end-user staff resources are allocated to the project. End users must be available to provide realistic feedback to the software developers throughout the design and implementation phases. Chapter 7 discusses management strategies that encourage active involvement and facilitate providing meaningful feedback to the developers.

Be cautious about including functions in the initial system that are *outside* your sphere of influence, particularly those for which:

1. cooperation is required from dissenting and noncommunicating groups;
2. management commitment cannot be ensured;
3. potential end users are skeptical and unenthusiastic.

When these situations are present within your area of authority, you have a variety of management options available to you, such as staff education and participation, staff transfer or reorganization, and increased management involvement and visibility. If these functions are within areas in which you have little or no management influence, such options are rarely available. End users who, for whatever reason, desire to see a computer system fail are in an extremely powerful position to ensure this fate.

Plan to build the system incrementally and start with a basic set of well-defined functions that together form a useful system. Do not allow needless complexity to creep into your system requirements. Simple systems have a much better chance of success. If the system is properly designed and makes use of the appropriate software development tools, it can be extended later with the added knowledge and experience gained through operational use. You are likely to face pressures—often from the systems development staff—to enlarge the scope of the system. Try not to be led astray by the glamour of the latest technology, and be particularly cautious when offered sophisticated solutions. The latest technology frequently offers good price-performance ratios and makes new things possible that could not be done earlier. However, technology for its own sake will not result in a system that meets your requirements. Keep in mind the roots of the word *sophisticated* when dealing with computer technology.

> *To sophisticate*, v.a.   To adulterate; to corrupt with something spurious.
>
> Samuel Johnson,
> *A Dictionary of the English Language*, 1755

> *Sophisticated*, adj.   1. Not in its natural or pure state; adulterated; amended unwarrantedly.   2. Deprived of native or original simplicity; made artificial or, more narrowly, highly complicated, refined, subtilized, etc.
>
> *Webster's New International Dictionary*, 1934

> *Sophisticate*, v.   To make impure or inferior by deceptively adding foreign substances.
>
> *Roget's II The New Thesaurus*, 1980

COST-BENEFIT TRADEOFFS

There would be few enterprises of great labour or hazard undertaken, if we had not the power of magnifying the advantages which we persuade ourselves to expect from them.

—Samuel Johnson,
The Rambler

You must carefully analyze costs and benefits to make the appropriate decisions regarding your system requirements.

Purchasing Off-the-Shelf Application Packages

An increasing variety of application software is available from commercial software vendors. Such packages may be purchased or leased, thereby saving the time required to develop a custom system. Many of these packages allow users to customize the software to meet their specific requirements. If you have gone through the process of identifying your system requirements and establishing the goals and objectives, you will have developed a solid basis for evaluating the available commercial software packages. Although these systems may not have been designed to meet your unique requirements, they often offer many advantages over custom-built software.

1. Software packages that have been in use for some time and in many different environments are likely to be thoroughly tested. Also, a vendor can afford to allocate more resources than a single customer can to maintenance and support of the product.
2. The functions supported in generalized packages may be extensive in order to meet the needs of a diverse user market. A package, therefore, may be more likely to meet your future requirements.

3. You will have the advantage of being able to discuss the strengths and weaknesses of the system with other users before you make a selection.

4. Commercial software vendors are under continuing market pressure to enhance and update their products. You will often benefit for little or no future cost. Serious vendors will have to update their products when legislation requires it, when new hardware becomes popular in their market, and when their competitors provide new capabilities. With custom-developed software, additional costs will be incurred when enhancements or updates are needed.

5. A widely used software package implicitly contains the influence of a broad base of user expertise and suggestions.

To discover which computer software is available for your application, consult one of the comprehensive software directories, such as *DataPro* or *Auerbach*. Directories are frequently divided into sections by major subject area, such as financial systems, manufacturing systems, and so forth. The listings usually include lease or purchase price, required hardware configuration, number of existing installations, and initial release date.

Narrow your selection to vendors with a good reputation in your application area who offer a system within your price range. Then develop a *Request for Proposal* based on your requirements, goals, and objectives. Be certain to include constraints that may apply, such as your existing or planned hardware environment. Many vendors will respond with a specific proposal that describes how their system will meet your needs, thus saving you considerable time laboring over their technical documentation to discover what their system can and cannot do. The time and care you devote to analyzing your system needs and developing specific requirements can be saved many times over when you receive vendor proposals that are written directly in response to your requirements.

To select among the vendor proposals, assign a weighting factor to each objective according to its importance. Devise a method for scoring the responses to each objective—for example, 5 points if software completely meets the objective, 3 for partially meets, 0 if does not meet at all. Assign each vendor a technical score within each

Requirement	Weight	Vendor A (Score x weight)	Vendor B (Score x weight)
1. Sales forecasting	20	3 x 20 = 60	5 x 20 = 100
2. Sales volume	20	5 x 20 = 100	3 x 20 = 60
3. Order processing speed	10	3 x 10 = 30	4 x 10 = 40
4. Operational costs	25	5 x 25 = 125	3 x 25 = 75
5. Lead processing	15	3 x 15 = 45	0 x 15 = 0
6. Surveys and analysis	10	0 x 10 = 0	3 x 10 = 30
Total Score	100	360	305

Figure 1: Software package evaluation

category, which is the total of the points in a category multiplied by the weight of the category. These technical scores can then be compared with the vendors' cost proposals and the available packages can be ranked.

The evaluation of software packages using this approach for the sales management system is shown in Figure 1.

Require the vendor to supply a list of current customer references, preferably including some in a similar industry and of a similar size to your own. Obtain the names of responsible personnel in both the end-user area and the computer system area. Arrange for a member of the computer staff in your organization to speak with her or his counterpart to discuss issues such as hardware and system compatibilities and computing resource requirements. Talk with your counterparts at current customer sites to determine their level of satisfaction with both the product and the vendor. Discuss any features that you find questionable or unclear. Find out their attitudes about the vendor's services in addition to the package's capabilities. Examples of some important service-related questions are listed below.

How responsive has the company been when problems have occurred?

- How quickly are problems resolved?
- Is there a 24-hour hotline for customer support?
- Is the documentation well written and accurate?

What is offered to facilitate customer training?

- Are courses available in-house or only in distant cities?
- Do the classes include workshops providing actual system experience?
- Are classes offered at frequent intervals?
- Does the system software include an interactive tutorial for user training?

How difficult was the package to install?

- How quickly was the system operational after its receipt?
- How much customer staff time was required for installation from end users and programmers?

Most vendors will provide their software for an initial trial period, say thirty days. Certain types of applications require substantial preparation and setup work, such as constructing a chart of accounts for a general ledger system or specifying benefit deduction options and amounts for a payroll system. If your application is one for which many decisions must be made and a considerable amount of work outside the system be completed before you can begin to use the software package, be certain that you understand what is required, and that you arrange for the trial period to begin after this work is completed.

Developmental Versus Operational Costs

The costs of your system should be viewed over a period extending several years beyond installation. The developmental costs and hardware purchases represent one-time expenditures. Operational costs are recurring and include charges for computer time, hardware maintenance and leases, operational staff, and maintenance programming.

Any savings that can be realized in the operational costs may justify increases in the developmental costs. You will need to estimate the projected life of the system and its associated hardware to establish reasonable tradeoffs between these types of costs. Much of this judgment will be based on the dynamic or static nature of your application, which will affect the length of time the system will continue to meet your requirements and the programming costs of future enhancements and maintenance. For example, if your system is likely to meet your needs for five years as opposed to two years, you can afford to invest more in the developmental effort in order to cut the longer-term operational costs. If many of the system parameters are subject to variability over time, it is probably worth additional developmental costs to provide the needed flexibility in the initial design rather than incurring continuing maintenance costs during the life of the system.

Often a computer system requires a large initial investment, but extensions to the system can be had for little additional cost. For example, additional memory and communication links may be required and terminal management software needed for a computer to support even one terminal. However, provided some hardware or software threshold is not exceeded, the expense of adding more terminals to the system may simply be the cost of each terminal. The costs of hardware, such as terminals and memory, continue to decrease while, at the same time, labor costs increase. As a result, the purchase of additional terminals to increase staff productivity and the purchase of additional memory to improve terminal response time are increasingly justifiable.

Chapter 3

DEFINE THE SYSTEM IN DATA TERMS

THE INPUT-PROCESS-OUTPUT MODEL

Three components are necessary to describe a process.

1. its inputs (raw materials, data, schedules);
2. its internal rules (how the inputs are turned into outputs);
3. its outputs (the end products of the process).

A functional description for a computer system can be divided into two major parts:

1. a data specification describing all the data inputs and outputs of the system;
2. a process specification explaining what operations must be performed on the inputs in order to produce the outputs.

Each function that should be included in the computer system can be described separately in terms of its inputs, outputs, and processing rules. The entire system, or any subset of it, can be viewed from this perspective. The outputs of each process are determined not only by its inputs but also by its processing instructions—that is, the rules by which certain outputs are produced when the process receives certain inputs. These rules can be viewed as the intelligence within the process, or what the process must know about the relationships between inputs and outputs. Within computer systems, this intelligence exists in the form of software (computer programs and data bases) or is contained in the hardware (physical devices and circuitry.) Those rules implemented through hardware solutions are generally faster to execute, but are more difficult and expensive to alter when the rules need to be changed. In most application systems, processing rules are contained within the software.

The system design should accommodate the level of change that is expected to occur in inputs, outputs, and processing rules. The design specification should include information related to the types of changes that are anticipated in the future. Changes also may occur in the hardware environment in which the software must function. Often changes that require an increase in processing speed or data storage capacity will necessitate changes in the hardware, such as additional computer memory, a faster computer, or larger capacity disk storage units. In order for the designers to plan for these changes in the initial design, information related to current and anticipated future needs should be included in the design specification.

The input-process-output approach to describing functions can be further applied to other levels of the system. The total system can be viewed as three subsystems, each one nested within the other, as in Figure 2.

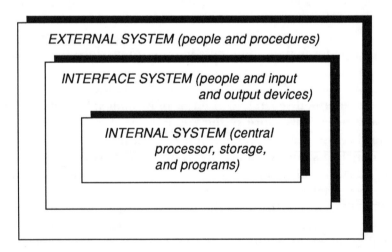

Figure 2: System levels

Each of the systems may contain many different processes, each with its own inputs and outputs. The systems communicate with each other through inputs and outputs, and the internal workings of each system do not have to be known outside it. Only the system inputs and outputs between adjacent systems are of consequence. The outputs of the *external system* are inputs to the *interface system* and so on, as shown in Figure 3.

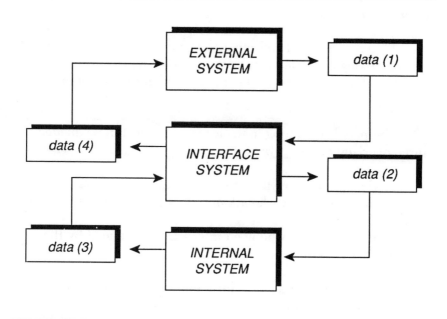

Figure 3: System data flow

THE EXTERNAL SYSTEM

The *external system* is the world outside the computer in which facts are generated and collected and where computer-generated information is interpreted and disseminated. The outputs of the external system are the facts and requests for information, shown together as data (1) in Figure 3. The external form of this data must be appropriate to the system operators in the external system—primarily the people who need to generate and understand this data. (In some cases, the production of data in the external system may be mechanized, such as data produced by a machine that takes temperature readings in a warehouse.) The input back to the external system is the information produced by the computer system, data (4) in Figure 3, and, again, it must be in the appropriate external form for the operators of the external system, such as people.

With respect to a computer system, the typical processes of the *external system* are:

1. generating and collecting *facts*;
2. asking *questions* about data in the system;
3. interpreting and disseminating computer-generated *information*.

The people operating in the *external system* can be divided into three overlapping categories:

1. data producers who generate the necessary *facts*;
2. data requesters who ask *questions* about previously entered facts;
3. data receivers who need *information* produced by the computer system.

If you begin your analysis by defining the outputs first and then using them to define the necessary inputs, you will develop the minimum set of required inputs. To follow this approach, first identify the group of people who need information. Then determine the form in which the information is needed, such as a printed report, terminal display, charts, graphs, or magnetic tape. By carefully defining the *questions* that the computer system must be able to answer, the overall scope of the computer system is determined. The computer system outputs that constitute answers to the questions become the starting point for determining which facts must be collected.

Within the input-process-output framework, each system component can be described separately. Begin by defining the final system outputs for each system component in terms of their data contents. For each data item included on a final output, determine its source

—"where does it come from?" A data item is either *derived* from combining other data items according to defined rules, or it is *raw input data*—that is, it must be entered into the computer directly. The rules themselves may contain additional data items, such as variables and constants, which are also either derived from or entered directly into the system.

By starting the analysis with the final output requirements and working backwards to determine the inputs, the raw input data will be all the data items that are both necessary and sufficient for the production of required outputs. This approach prevents the inclusion of unnecessary data, while at the same time ensures that required input data is not omitted. The data collection function is often the most expensive component of automated systems and therefore should be approached conservatively.

Once the set of raw input data is determined for all functions, the relationships that exist among these data items must be described. How do the data items relate in the real world? Group together those data items that relate to the same real-world unit or event, such as customer-name, customer-address, customer-type-of-business. Identify data items whose values depend on the values of other data items, such as customer-discount-rate, which depends on customer-status and year-to-date-customer-sales. Identify the external format of each raw input data item. For example, customer-name is one to fifty characters; customer-status is coded either 1 for wholesale or 2 for retail; and product-number is a ten-character identifier, the first three of which indicate the product line, the next three define the product, and the last four identify the specific version or release of the product.

A summary of the system data flow for the *external system* is shown in Figure 4.

THE INTERFACE SYSTEM

The *interface system* is where data inputs are converted from external to internal form and where data outputs are changed from internal to external form. The *facts* are collected in their external form, such as a sales order, and through a system input device, such as a terminal or optical scanner, are converted to a machine-sensible form. The *questions* as they are formulated in the external system—such as

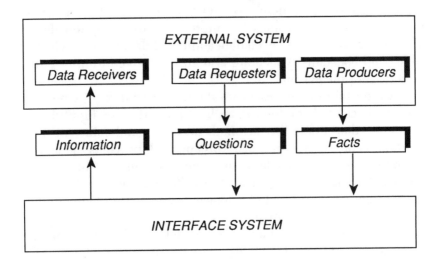

Figure 4: External system data flow

"What are next quarter's sales likely to be?"—must be translated into suitable inquiries that can be understood by the internal process that generates the computer outputs, say a request for the sales forecast report. The machine-sensible translations of facts and questions into input sets and inquiries are shown as data (3) in Figure 3. The translations of computer-produced data into the appropriate external form of information are shown as data (4) in Figure 3.

For the interface system, the facts are generally grouped into related sets of raw input data items. For example, all the data related to a customer order could be grouped on a single source form and entered as one input set, commonly called a *transaction*. Data collected from prospective employees could be grouped on an employment application form and entered as one input set. Each input set (transaction) must be converted from its external to internal form. The data conversion process may take place *off-line*, as on a key-to-tape machine, or *on-line*, as on a video-terminal. *Off-line* means that the conversion device is not connected to the computer in which the data will be processed and where previously entered data is stored.

On-line data entry affords considerably more capabilities to verify the accuracy of input data, since the data in each transaction can be compared for consistency with data previously stored on the computer files. For example, the customer-number on an order can be checked against the customer-master-file. If the customer-number does not exist, the computer can alert the person entering the transaction of the possibility that the customer-number may have been typed incorrectly. Verifying the accuracy of the customer-number just entered is much easier when the sales order is still in front of the person. If these transactions were converted in an off-line process, the error would be detected by the computer later and someone would need to find the sales order in question, possibly by looking through a large stack of sales orders.

Frequently the data receivers are not people; instead they may be other software systems on the same or different computers. For example, one division of a company may need to send sales data to the corporate system, or the sales system may need to send data to the general ledger system. Magnetic tapes are commonly used, since well-defined industry standards exist, to transfer data from one computer to another when the two have no communication links. Magnetic tapes may also be an intermediate form of output, such as when data must be transferred to another device for microfiche production or phototypesetting.

Interactiveness

In defining specifications for the interface system, you need to specify the degree of interactiveness that you want the system to have. This characteristic can be thought of in the same way as other forms of communication. If two people have only one form of communication, such as writing letters, available to them, then their communication has a low degree of interactiveness. Conversely, if they can communicate by telephone or in person, their communication is highly interactive. The basic factors involved are:

1. the size of the communication units,
2. the elapsed time before feedback.

In letter writing, the communication units may be large—for example, entire letters discussing many topics. The elapsed time before feedback is relatively long: the time required for mail to travel in each direction plus the time to compose a response to each letter. In telephone or face-to-face communication, the units are relatively small: single topics, sentences, or words; and the elapsed time before feedback is quite short. Even so, if the size of communication units is ridiculously small (single words or syllables) the feedback is disruptive. Clearly, too frequent feedback would interfere with the communication process itself. Depending on the nature of the communication, a reasonable size unit should be sent, say several sentences, before pausing for feedback. The degree of interactiveness that is desirable is related to the nature and purpose of the communication. A lecturer may want to present an entire topic before stopping for questions and comments from the audience. The easiest method of describing the degree of interactiveness for computer system interfaces is to define the size of the communication units (a character, a data item, a transaction, a batch of transactions) and the acceptable elapsed time before feedback (a millisecond, a minute, an hour).

A highly interactive system is one in which an end user enters a small amount of data and receives an instant response. The degree of interactiveness decreases when the amount of data entered prior to receiving feedback is larger, or when the elapsed time before feedback is longer. Too frequent feedback will tend to interfere with fast and efficient input by high-volume, experienced end users, although they will appreciate a quick response after the data is entered. Conversely, the casual and inexperienced end user is more likely to benefit from frequent feedback that reassures that the data is being entered properly. The system should tailor the level and timing of the feedback to suit the task and the characteristics of the end user. The way in which the system solicits data should also be tailored to the end user. Systems that require frequent and experienced end users to wade through several levels of menu selection quickly become frustrating, but presenting novice end users with a clear presentation of possible choices in a structured way can be helpful. Further discussion of specific techniques for interacting with different types of end users is presented in Chapter 8.

Batch Interfaces

A *batch mode* of input simply means that transactions are presented to computer processing in batches, which in turn generates batches of outputs, which may then be presented as inputs to another process, and so on. Processes done in batch mode typically require fewer computer resources because less computer time is devoted to overhead functions such as initiating and terminating processes (scheduling). More computer resources can be used for actual processing of data. Batch mode, however, may not make the most efficient use of *external system* resources, such as data entry staff, and often it is advantageous to use computer resources for such overhead functions when faster response times would improve staff productivity. The higher development and ongoing computer costs may be easily justified by lower recurring staff costs.

Batch mode processes have a low degree of interactiveness, since an entire batch of inputs is entered before any feedback, such as an error report, is provided. For inputs requiring more timely feedback, an on-line interface is appropriate. For each type of transaction, you should specify what types of processing are required to provide the necessary feedback. Transactions may only require simple checks for valid data, such as "are the contents numeric," and the remainder of the processing may be done in batch mode. Other transactions may require more extensive on-line processing, such as verifying an employee-number with the payroll master file.

A batch interface may, in fact, be highly automated—one method uses an optical scanner that converts typewritten documents to machine-sensible data. Such a process may be done using a microcomputer, but the interface is *off-line* if there is no access to the computer in which subsequent processing of the data occurs.

On-Line Interfaces

Batch interfaces do not necessarily meet requirements for rapid response time. Since computer hardware costs have been decreasing dramatically while labor costs have been rising, on-line interfaces are increasingly easy to cost-justify. On-line entry of both raw input and inquiries should be considered.

Inquiries. For each inquiry that must be entered on-line, you should determine how much processing should be done in on-line mode.

1. Should the inquiry simply be received and stored for later processing?
2. Should the inquiry be checked for input errors and feasibility?
3. Should the requested output be produced immediately?

Determine what types of inquiries will be made. Will the inquiries be limited to requesting the display of predefined reports? In this case the end user can be presented with a menu of available reports and make a selection. Both the data contents and the report format must have been previously defined within the system if this approach is chosen. If more flexibility at the time of request is required, then a more complex inquiry process will be necessary. The end user will need to enter the specific *recipes* describing the format and contents of the desired output. In this case, a menu approach will not suffice. The capability to receive and translate ad hoc inquiries is often available through generalized software packages such as on-line inquiry and report-writer components of data base management systems. Developing a customized capability for this function is generally expensive, and, in addition, there are advantages to using one general purpose inquiry language to access many application systems. Staff may learn one language and apply this skill to many different application systems, and the costs of acquiring such software can be shared by many users.

Since the capability to produce outputs in an on-line mode will require more computer resources than are necessary to simply receive and check for errors in the data, you may choose to limit the number and types of outputs actually displayed on-line. A compromise might be to allow the request to be made on-line, have the outputs prepared in batch-mode, and then allow on-line requests for display of these already prepared outputs. This choice is especially appropriate for outputs that require lengthy processing, and it avoids using the additional computing resources required for increased on-line processing.

The *information* needs of the external system may be satisfied by several different types of outputs:

1. outputs that are predefined and scheduled;
2. outputs that are predefined and *on request*;
3. outputs that are partially predefined and require other variables to be supplied by the end user at the time of request;
4. outputs that are not defined until the time of request.

Input Transactions. For each transaction that will be entered in on-line mode, specify how much processing will be done on-line:

1. Should the input simply be entered on-line?
2. How much data validation should be performed on-line?
3. Should the master files be updated on-line?

Simple and absolute data item validation (for example, checking that employee-hours-worked contains a numeric quantity, or that employee-sex is M or F) will not require significant computing resources. Certain types of relative data validation may also be feasible, such as checking the consistency of data being entered on the same transaction. Checking consistency between the new data and data already stored on the computer files requires additional computing resources and may not be feasible on small computers. Its feasibility depends on the size of the existing data base, the efficiency with which that data base can be accessed, and the complexity of the data validation requirement. For example, does the data need to be checked against the contents of one data record or that of fifty different records?

End users must understand that if they request outputs that require lengthy processing to be prepared on-line it can interfere with response time for other apparently unrelated processes. Consider a system that supports high-volume data entry of sales orders and products shipped. Assume that once the input data on each transaction is validated, the customer master file is updated. If a sales manager is permitted to request an on-line report of average sales amount on order but not yet shipped, further on-line entry of these transactions will need to be suspended until the report is prepared so that the average will be accurate for a point in time. The processing required to produce this average necessitates reading each record of the master file and subtracting the total amount of products shipped from the total amount ordered. The differences are summed across all customers and divided by the number of customers. If further updating is permitted once the summing process begins, the average computed will not represent the average at the time of the request or at the time of the display, since a record already read may be further changed and a record may be changed before it is read by the program computing the average. Although the accuracy of the output may not be a critical issue in this example, it can often be one in complex multi-user systems.

In on-line systems with multiple, simultaneous end users, careful consideration must be given to how the on-line functions will interact. To the extent that lengthy processes are not performed in on-line mode, the interference can be minimized. Another technique for dealing with this problem is to periodically create an abbreviated file containing the type of information commonly requested, and permit inquiries against the data on that file instead of directly against the master file. The use of a shortened file will permit faster responses to inquiries, and the file can be recreated with the latest data from the master file at various time intervals, such as daily, weekly, or monthly.

Some batch interfaces are usually required in large systems even if all the functions are also available on-line. Certain types of output may not be suitable for terminal display (special graphics, microfiche), or permanent printed copy may be required. The end user may receive large-volume printed outputs faster by producing them on a high-speed printer in batch mode rather than on a slow typewriter terminal in on-line mode.

Real-Time Interfaces

When the computer system is directly interacting with real-world events at the actual time they occur, it is called a *real-time interface*. Such systems must be able to perform all necessary internal processing while keeping up with the external events as they occur. Typically, such computers are dedicated to monitoring one set of external processes; they are often analog rather than digital computers, which means that data is in the form of continuously varying rather than digitized electrical signals. Data collected by real-time systems may later be processed on general-purpose digital computers.

If the computer system must monitor or control an external process directly, such as operating a machine on an assembly line, then timing is of critical importance and a shared multi-user system is unlikely to be a suitable environment. Design specifications for real-time systems require detailed temporal descriptions of the real-world events that must be monitored or controlled by the computer.

In summary, the *interface* system has two parts. The input conversion component converts the *facts* and *questions* into machine-sensible *input sets* (transactions) and *inquiries* for processing by the internal system. The output component of the interface system converts the machine-sensible data, data (3) in Figure 3, to the appropriate external form of *information*, data (4) in Figure 3.

THE INTERNAL SYSTEM

The internal system processes its inputs—raw data and inquiries—according to the specifications contained in the software programs. The outputs produced by the internal system contain three types of data:

1. **raw data**   data entered into the computer and stored in computer files or memory

2. **derived data**   data generated by the computer from the *raw input* and the programmed *rules*, such as sums, averages, and ratios.

3. **error data**   data entered in *raw input* or *inquiries* that was detected as errors and should be reentered.

Typical processes in the internal system are:

1. Input validation
2. Data storage and retrieval
3. Data derivation
4. Output formatting

A SUMMARY OF SYSTEM INPUTS AND OUTPUTS

Figure 5 presents a summary of the three systems and the flow of inputs and outputs among them.

From the model shown in Figure 5, the questions that should be answered during the analysis phase can be determined.

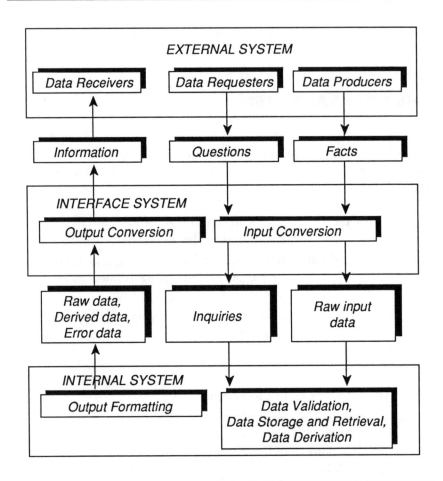

Figure 5: Input-process-output model

ANALYSIS QUESTIONS TO BE ANSWERED

For the external system:

1. What information is required by the data receivers?
2. What reports can be predefined to provide this information?
   A. What are the data items in each report?
   B. What is the appropriate external format?
   C. Which reports should be produced according to pre-defined schedules or external events?
   D. Which reports are to be produced on request?
      a. What is the estimated frequency of request?
      b. How quickly must they be produced after a request?
3. What end-user capabilities are needed to define new reports?
   A. What parameters can the end user supply?
   B. What is the estimated frequency of requests?
   C. How quickly must the reports be produced after a request?
4. Are any special external distribution procedures needed to disseminate output from point of generation to destination?
5. For data items that cannot be derived and therefore must be entered into the system, how will these facts be collected and grouped into transactions for data entry?
   A. Which facts are generated at the same time?
   B. Which facts are generated by the same data producer?
   C. Which facts refer to the same external entity, such as employee, customer, or department?

For the interface system:

6. What are the transactions containing the raw input data items?
   A. By what method should each be converted to machine-sensible form: on-line or off-line?
   B. What is the volume and frequency of each type of transaction?
   C. How quickly must detected errors be reported?
   D. What external processes may be required to determine how to correct detected errors?

  E. What security measures apply to each type of trans-
    action?
    a. Which staff are allowed to enter each type of trans-
      action?
    b. Under what conditions are additional authorizations
      required?
    c. Under what conditions should exception reports be
      produced?
 7. What on-request inquiries are permitted?
  A. How often will each request be made?
  B. What volume of output will result from each type of
    request?
  C. Will the inquiry be made on-line or off-line?
  D. Should the output be displayed on-line?
  E. If errors are detected in the inquiry, how quickly must
    they be reported?
  F. What security measures apply to each type of inquiry?
    a. Which staff are allowed to make each type of inquiry?
    b. Are the output results to be restricted to a subset of
      available data?
    c. Under what conditions should exception reports be
      produced?

For the internal system:

 8. What are the permissible values for each data item (numeric
   ranges, a value contained in a set of predefined codes, such
   as a table of valid state abbreviations)?
 9. What relationships must be maintained among the data items
   (quantity-shipped should be less than or equal to quantity-
   ordered)?
10. What actions (e.g., audit trails, exception reports, supervisory notification) are required when files are updated?
11. What is the active life of the data?
  A. Under what conditions can data be automatically purged?
  B. Under what conditions can historical data be summa-
    rized or stored in less accessible archival form, such as
    microfiche or magnetic tape?

12. How sensitive, proprietary, or confidential is the data?
    A. Does the operating system provide adequate security, or will additional measures be necessary?
    B. Are passwords sufficient to control terminal access, or will additional provisions be necessary?
    C. Should the data be stored in encrypted form?
13. How quickly must the system be back in operation after a malfunction or catastrophic event?
    A. What is an acceptable period of data loss: an hour, a day, a week?
    B. If the system is crucial to the organization, what are the acceptable alternatives during a disaster recovery: alternate computing sites, reversion to manual processes?
14. What are the rules to be used for deriving each data item (computations, encoding and decoding tables, comparisons and relationships)?

The objective of the systems analysis phase is to provide the answers to these questions. Part 2 presents a general approach to the systems analysis phase and a ten-step plan using this approach to complete the analysis and prepare a requirements definition.

Part Two

HOW TO DEVELOP
SYSTEM SPECIFICATIONS

Our life is frittered away by detail . . .
   Simplify, simplify.

—Henry David Thoreau,
   Walden 2

Chapter 4

FIND STRUCTURES
THAT SIMPLIFY

A TOP-DOWN APPROACH TO SYSTEMS ANALYSIS

The approach to problem definition presented in this section is simple and straightforward, but nonetheless powerful. Nothing in the approach itself is computer related; it simply facilitates the structuring of problems so that solutions are more easily obtainable. This approach is especially applicable to the design specification tasks since it separates problem definition from problem solution. As applied to design specification, the approach inherently facilitates the following tasks:

1. development of detailed requirements that are both necessary and sufficient for devising suitable solutions;
2. development of a logical and relational structure in which detailed requirements can be expressed, understood, and unambiguously communicated;
3. development of an integrated specification to facilitate analysis of the implications of subsequent design decisions;
4. clear separation of tasks associated with design specification from those associated with the design phase.

Each of these inherent properties lessens the probability that the more common mistakes, such as the following, will occur in the specifications:

1. Some requirements are omitted inadvertently.
2. Some requirements are not explicitly stated and must be inferred.
3. Some requirements are inappropriately stated and unnecessarily overconstrain design solutions.

4. The impacts of subsequent design decisions on stated requirements cannot be assessed effectively.

The top-down approach not only addresses the specific problems encountered in developing design specifications; it also addresses some general sentiments about tackling important, complex problems:

1. The problem seems large and overwhelming.
2. Where to begin is unclear.
3. The large number of minor details is distracting.
4. The problem seems to enlarge in scope as attempts at definition are made, and the lack of any sense of progress toward completion is frustrating.
5. The relationships among the parts of the problem are unclear.

These sentiments may be commonly felt by those developing design requirements, but such feelings are not limited to this area. The top-down approach can be used for a variety of tasks where one or more of these characteristics apply.

Stated simply, the top-down approach divides a problem into two or more smaller problems that together are equivalent to the first. Each of the resulting problems is then broken down into four or more smaller problems, and so on, as shown in Figure 6.

As more problems are created, the scope of each becomes smaller and therefore easier to define.

As the breakdown continues, the scope of each problem becomes progressively smaller and therefore easier to define. The scope of the original problem remains unchanged, provided that in the beginning it is both well-stated and complete. The set of resultant problems at the final step should be easier to solve. At each step of the breakdown, the set of resultant problem statements must be equivalent to the one from which it was created. If the breakdown meets this criterion at each step, then solving the final set of smaller problems solves the original problem. Using Figure 6 as an example, problem 1-A and 1-B together equal problem 1: 2-A and 2-B together equal problem 2; and finally, problem 1 and 2 together equal the original problem.

The approach will provide not only a set of more manageable problems but also a logical and relational context in which to view

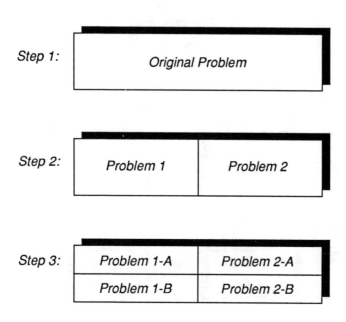

Figure 6: A top-down approach

the individual solutions; therefore, the structure of the breakdown process itself should be retained. The simple problem task shown in Figure 7 illustrates how the structure of the breakdown shows the relationships among the parts and to the whole.

The breakdowns do not have to be symmetric. Each breakdown may generate a different number of lower-level problem statements. Nor does the process have to be applied in parallel across one level. One branch of the tree can be further broken down any number of levels before breaking down another branch. The criterion is that the statements at each new level are together equivalent to the one from which they were generated.

Any dimension can be used to divide the problem into smaller ones; however, the dimension should be one that suits the nature of

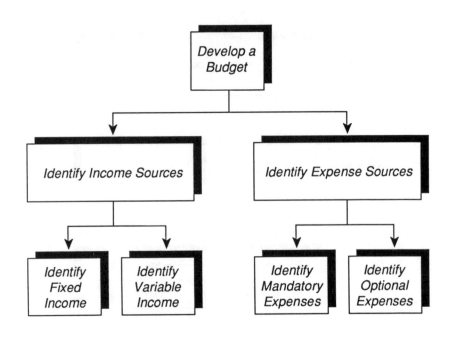

Figure 7: A top-down budget development structure

the problem statement. In Figure 7, the first-level breakdown uses the natural components of a budget: income and expenses. The second-level breakdown for income uses type-of-income—fixed and variable—while expenses were divided into mandatory and optional. The dimension used in one breakdown may be different from the ones used in others. Helpful dimensions to use for breaking the problem down have the following properties:

1. Meaningful relationships are illuminated among the resultant smaller problems.
2. The resultant problems are simpler than the ones from which they were generated, and the process can continue if necessary.

Finding a helpful dimension to use at each step is a trial-and-error process. If the breakdown fails to yield simpler problems or meaningful information about problem relationships, such as dependencies, independencies, interdependencies, similarities, differences, and the like, then retry that step using a different dimension for the breakdown. If the resulting problems are almost as large as their predecessors, with one or two trivial modifications, little progress has been made.

The check for completeness at each step is critical to the successful application of this top-down approach. Choosing a known dimension along which to break down each problem is useful in testing completeness. For example, for problems involving processes, useful dimensions are often *time* or *type* of function. The *time* dimension is most useful when chronological order is an important relationship, that is, one that affects the end results. The *type* dimension varies with the nature of the problem, but can be generally described as a characteristic that distinguishes one component from another, such as income and expense as two types of budget components, fixed and variable as two types of income, mandatory and optional as two types of expenses. The resulting breakdowns should cover the full range of the chosen dimension if the problem breakdowns at each level are to be complete.

Although the top-down approach does not itself solve the original problem, it simplifies it by transforming it into a set of smaller problems that can then be solved more easily. For example, if the original problem requires a decision to be made, then after the top-down approach is applied, a series of smaller decisions will need to be made. If the problem has been broken down in appropriate ways, then each one of these decisions can be made within a meaningful context. The effect of each decision on the others will be evident.

Before delving into the application of top-down problem decomposition for analyzing software system requirements, a simple example of the use of this technique for planning a menu for a dinner party is presented in Figure 8.

The first-level breakdown uses the time dimension. Subsequent breakdowns use type of food and beverages served at each time—before dinner, during dinner, and after dinner. Although the specific menu has not been determined as yet by this process, it has been reduced to sixteen smaller decisions, such as *choose meat entrees,*

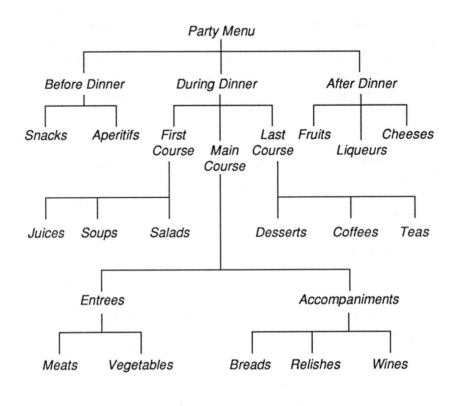

Figure 8: A top-down structure for a party menu

choose vegetable entrees, choose soups. The structure of the break-down also indicates which items will be served together and therefore should be compatible. At this point the problem is defined and so-lutions can be easily devised and evaluated. You select a logical start-ing point, such as the *entrees* for the *main course,* and proceed to make each decision.

If different dimensions or a different order for the breakdowns is used, the same set of final decisions may result. But the relationships shown by the structure will be different. In Figure 9, the breakdown

First Breakdown by **time**:	First Breakdown by **type**:
Before Dinner	Food
Snacks	Appetizers
Aperitifs	Snacks
At Dinner	Soups
First Course	Salads
Juices	Entrees
Soups	Meats
Salads	Vegetables
Main Course	Accompaniments
Entrees	Breads
Meats	Relishes
Vegetables	Desserts
Accompaniments	Fruits
Breads	Cheeses
Relishes	Beverages
Last Course	Spirits
Desserts	Aperitifs
Coffees	Wines
Teas	Liqueurs
After Dinner	Non Spirits
Fruits	Juices
Cheeses	Coffees
Liqueurs	Teas

Figure 9: Two structures for a menu plan

used in Figure 8 is shown in the left column and a new one is shown in the right column.

The final set of decisions is the same; however, the left column facilitates the choosing of complementary items when they will be served together. The right column fails to show this relationship among the items and is thus more likely to be incomplete.

Each step of any breakdown should be done using a single identifiable and meaningful dimension. The number of intermediate levels
does not increase the scope of the final problems, but it does help
point out important relationships among the final set and aids their
solution by placing them in a meaningful context.

The use of this technique permits many of the details to be
ignored until the problem is well structured. Attempts to deal with
a myriad of minor details too early in the problem definition process
can often obscure the major components of the problem. The point
in the structure at which these details become relevant can be determined by assessing the scope of effect of each one. If the detail
affects all the breakdowns below a certain level, then the detail should
be noted at that level. For example, the number of guests at the party
will affect the required quantity of every menu item; therefore, this
detail should be noted at the top level. If a guest is known to have
an allergy to certain citrus products, this detail could be noted at the
level of fruits and juices. After all the details have been noted, implementing a solution can begin.

Some of the common obstacles to problem solving were presented earlier in this chapter. They are repeated here, together with
an explanation of how the top-down approach can help in overcoming
each one.

1. *The problem seems large and overwhelming.*

   This approach simplifies the problem by breaking it into smaller
   ones that are individually less formidable.

2. *Where to begin is unclear.*

   This approach provides a structure in which a logical starting
   point and path through the structure can be found.

3. *The large number of minor details is distracting.*

   This approach permits the details to be ignored until the
   breakdowns reach a level at which they are relevant; the
   logical structure of the top-down model also provides a context in which to evaluate where such details apply.

4. *The problem seems to enlarge in scope as attempts at solution
   are made, and the lack of any sense of progress toward completion is frustrating.*

The scope of each problem at each new level is smaller, and the solutions may be deferred until the entire structure is developed. As each part of the problem is solved, what remains to be done can be more easily seen.

5. *The relationships among the various parts of the problem are unclear.*

The intermediate levels of the structure serve to illuminate meaningful relationships that may not have been evident before.

The top-down approach can make defining your system requirements much easier. It does not, however, substitute for knowledge of the subject at hand or the ability to gather the relevant facts. The technique should be applied creatively and with careful thought. In situations where it does not appear to help in defining requirements, do not become needlessly bound by it.

Knowledge is of two kinds: we know a subject ourselves, or we know where we can find information upon it.

—Samuel Johnson,
Boswell's *Life of Johnson*

AN OVERVIEW OF AN ANALYSIS PLAN

When using the top-down approach defining system requirements, the first-level breakdown is likely to be major functional areas. The sales management system discussed in Part 1 would be broken down as in Figure 10.

A functional system breakdown, such as the one shown in Figure 10, can be combined with the input-process-output system model developed in Chapter 3. Each subfunction can be separately defined by applying the input-process-output model to create a second-level

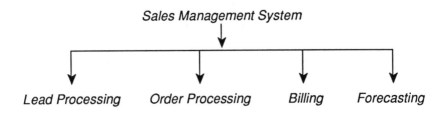

Figure 10: A top-down structure for a sales management system

breakdown, shown as Functional Breakdown Model in Figure 11. Alternatively, each system layer can be defined using each subfunction as the second-level breakdown, shown as Input-Process-Output Model in Figure 11. Each of the subfunctions may be further broken down into their subcomponents, for example, Order Processing may consist of Order Entry, Inventory Update, and Shipping. Figure 11 shows these two possible breakdowns of a sales management system.

Breaking down both the functional and the input-process-output system models has, in each case, yielded twelve subsystems to define. In both models, the primary focus of the external system section is to define the external system in terms of data items and specify what information must be produced by the computer system. The interface system section specifies the processes that are required to convert input data and inquiries from their external to their internal form and back, particularly how the software is to interface with the end users. The internal system section describes what processes are needed for input validation, file updating, file backup and recovery, data security, output data derivation, and report formatting.

The next section presents a brief overview of ten steps that will result in a requirements definition. These ten steps cover each of the three system layers: external, interface, and internal. Using the functional breakdown of the sales management system in Figure 11 as an example, these steps need to be completed for each of the four subsystems: lead processing, order processing, billing, and forecasting.

Functional Breakdown Model	Input-Process-Output Model

A. Lead Processing System
  1. External System
  2. Interface System
  3. Internal System
B. Order Processing System
  1. External System
  2. Interface System
  3. Internal System
C. Billing System
  1. External System
  2. Interface System
  3. Internal System
D. Forecasting System
  1. External System
  2. Interface System
  3. Internal System
	A. External System
	  1. Lead Processing
	  2. Order Processing
	  3. Billing System
	  4. Forecasting System
	B. Interface System
	  1. Lead Processing
	  2. Order Processing
	  3. Billing System
	  4. Forecasting System
	C. Internal System
	  1. Lead Processing
	  2. Order Processing
	  3. Billing System
	  4. Forecasting System

Figure 11: Subsystems of a sales management system

External System Tasks

Step 1: Define information needs

The goal of this task is to produce a complete list of all system data items. To begin, examine all the questions the computer system must be able to answer. What are the *subjects* of the questions—employees, customers, accounts, products, and so forth? What type of information is required for each subject? What data items make up this information?

Step 2: Determine required inputs

Separate the data items developed in step 1 into two categories by determining which ones can be derived from others and which ones must be supplied to the system.

Step 3:Define data relationships

Describe how the data items relate to each other. Which ones refer to the same subject? For example, which items refer to employees, which ones to customers? Group together data items that have the same determining variables to form input sets within each subject data base.

Interface System Tasks

Step 4: Define computer outputs

List sets of computer-produced outputs that will satisfy predefined information needs. Each output should be described in terms of the data items contained within it, the sequence and format in which it should be presented, and the mode of presentation, such as terminal display or printed copy. If the output is to be produced on a scheduled basis, define that schedule and other related requirements. The use of a prototype, such as a sample page of a report or a sample screen display, is the simplest method to communicate your output needs to the software developers.

Step 5: Define inquiry capabilities

Gather the following information about those outputs that are not produced automatically on a schedule or those that do not have predefined contents or formats. How often will the requests be made? How soon after the request will the output be needed? What security provisions are necessary? What type of end user will make the request—(one who uses the system often or only occasionally)?

Step 6: Identify sources of inputs

Using the information gathered in steps 2 and 3, determine where and in what form the required inputs will be collected. Group the related input items based on their common sources, frequencies, and the subjects to which they apply, such as customers, employees, or products. These groups of input data items form transactions. Gather data related to volumes and frequencies for each transaction type.

Step 7: Define data-entry procedures

Using the information gathered in step 6, determine the requirements for data entry support. For those transactions involving on-line data entry, specify the level and type of computer assistance required to support the data-entry process. For example, specify whether the end users will typically be experienced with the system and will be entering large volumes of data on a routine basis, or casual users of the system who will need well-structured prompting from the software about which data items should be entered, and will require frequent feedback from the system concerning the validity of their input.

Internal System Tasks

Step 8: Specify data validation requirements

For each input data item, specify the possible range of values. Also, specify any consistency that should be maintained among the data items. Specify which kinds of data validation must be done at time of data-entry during later processing. Decide what information should be presented on error reports to facilitate the correction process.

Step 9: Define data protection requirements

Decide whether or not security measures are required for restricting access to the data base. Is the data highly sensitive? What costs are reasonable to ensure restriction of access to the data base? Determine how extensive backup and recovery procedures should be. How quickly must the system be operational after a power failure or a fire? Should alternative computing sites be sought for backup?

Step 10: Specify data derivation rules

Document the functional methods, formulas, mappings, and so forth that are to be used to produce derived data items. Choose a form for these rules that communicates the methods most straightforwardly.

The resulting information from these ten steps can be organized in any number of ways. One possible outline for a requirements

Requirements Definition

I.   *External System Description*

A. *Background and Rationale*
1. *Results of Needs Assessment*
2. *Definition of System Scope*
3. *System Goals and Objectives*
4. *Relationships to Other Systems*

B. *Constraints and Limitations*
1. *Required Hardware Compatibility*
2. *Required Software Compatibility*
3. *Developmental Budgets and Schedules*
4. *Operational and Maintenance Budgets and Schedules*

C. *Data Description*
1. *Definition of Required Inputs*
2. *Description of Data Relationships*
3. *Sources of Required Inputs*
4. *Input Schedules, Volumes, and Frequencies*
5. *Data Collection and Correction Procedures*

D. *Information Requirements*
1. *Description of Computer-produced Outputs*
2. *Output Schedules, Volumes, and Frequencies*
3. *Output Distribution Procedures*

II. *Interface System Description*

A. *Data-Entry Procedures*
1. *Mode of Entry*
2. *Level and Type of Computer Assistance*
3. *Response-time Requirements*
4. *Security Considerations and Other Controls*

Figure 12: Outline of a requirements definition

B. *Inquiry Capabilities*
    1. *Mode of Entry*
    2. *Level and Type of Computer Assistance*
    3. *Response-time Requirements*
    4. *Security Considerations and Other Controls*

III. *Internal System Description*

A. *Data Validation and Error Reporting Requirements*
B. *Data Base Protection and Recovery*
C. *Data Derivation Procedures*

IV. *Other Requirements*

A. *End-user Training*
B. *System Documentation Requirements*
C. *Development Standards*
D. *System Conversion Requirements*

V. *Optional Features and Future Extensions*

Figure 12: Continued

definition is shown in Figure 12. Such a document is also known as a *functional specification*, an *external system design*, or a *design specification*. It may also serve as a *request for proposal* to a vendor of a software system.

Each of the ten steps presented in this chapter is further described in Chapter 5 with specific examples of the use of the top-down approach in systems analysis.

Chapter 5

TEN STEPS TO A REQUIREMENTS DEFINITION

This chapter discusses each of the ten steps leading to a system requirements definition. Each section includes an example using the top-down approach.

The external system model is summarized in Figure 13.

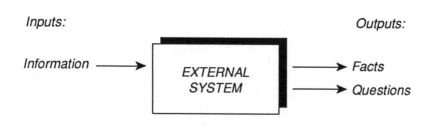

Figure 13: External system model

Step 1: Define Information Needs

Method: Determine the questions the computer system must be able to answer and define the answers in terms of data items.

This task may be viewed as a continuation of the needs assessment, but focusing on information needs. The information needs must be refined to the level of the individual data items that satisfy these

Financial Reporting System Information Needs

Internal Corporate Needs

   Management Needs
      Administration Department
      Marketing Department
      Personnel Department
      Research and Development Department
      Manufacturing Department
      Sales Department

   Employee Needs
      Profit-sharing Participant
      Stock Purchase Plan Participant
      Retirement Fund Participant

External Reporting Needs

   Board of Directors
      Finance Committee
      General Board

   Federal Agency Needs
      Internal Revenue Service
      Department of Commerce
      Securities and Exchange Commission

   State Agency Needs
      State-of-business
      State-of-sales

Figure 14: A top-down structure for analyzing information needs

needs—that is, the set of data items that taken together answer the questions.

A useful dimension for breaking down the information needs is often *type of data requester*. The top levels can be broadly defined and become successively more specific until the level is reached where individual data item requirements can be identified. Figure 14 is an example of such a decomposition for a financial reporting system.

Step 2: Determine Required Inputs

Method: Using the list of required output data items from step 1, determine which ones cannot be derived from others and, therefore, must be supplied to the system.

For each unique output data item identified in step 1, determine its type: *raw input* or *derived data*. For each derived data item, determine what data items are required in order to generate it. For example, employee-monthly-gross-pay is derived from several data items: employee-hours-worked, employee-sick-hours, employee-vacation-hours, employee-holiday-hours, and employee-hourly-rate. This process may in turn generate new data items for the list, for each of which you will again have to determine its type and, for those that can be derived, the data items from which it is generated. Continue this process until all the necessary *raw* data items have been identified. These data items constitute the required inputs to the system.

A useful dimension for a top-down breakdown is the *subject* referred to by the data item. Figure 15 illustrates a structure for defining the data items required for derivations. The *subjects* of the data items form the primary headings, and data items are listed below each heading. If the data item can be derived from other data items, the other required data items are shown beneath it. Those data items that cannot be further broken down form the *raw input data items* and are those that must be entered into the computer system.

A list of data items such as those generated above must then be studied to determine which of them can be derived from other data items and which must be supplied to the system as *raw input data items*. The data items that must be supplied to the system are the subject of the next step.

A. *Employee-Educational-Background*
   Year-of-Degree
   Type-of-Degree
   Major-Subject
   School-Name

B. *Employee-Work-Experience*
   Previous-Employment-Start-Date
   Previous-Employment-End-Date
   Previous-Employer-Name
   Previous-Employment-Title
   Previous-Employment-Ending-Salary

C. *Employee-Demographic-Information*
   Employee-Sex
   Employee-Date-of-Birth
   Employee-Racial-Classification
   Employee-Military-Status
   Employee-Handicap-Status

D. *Employee-W2-Report*
   Annual-Gross-Pay
   Annual-Withheld-Pay
   Annual-Sick-Pay
   Social-Security-Number
   Tax-Status
   Number-of-Exemptions

E. *Departmental-Payroll-Expense-Report*
   Employee-Department-Number
   Total-Regular-Pay
      Hourly-Rate
      Monthly

Figure 15: A top-down structure for analyzing required inputs

       Total-Overtime-Pay
        Regular-Hours
          Employment-Classification
          Monthly-Overtime-Hours
       Total-Vacation-Pay
        Hourly-Rate
        Monthly-Vacation-Hours
       Total-Sick-Pay
        Hourly-Rate
        Monthly-Sick-Hours

F. Employee-Pay-Checks
       Employee-Name
       Social-Security-Number
       Monthly-Net-Pay
        Monthly-Gross-Pay
         Hourly-Rate
         Overtime-Rate
          Employment-Classification
          Monthly-Overtime-Hours
         Monthly-Hours-Worked
          Monthly-Regular-Hours
          Monthly-Overtime-Hours
         Monthly-Leave-Hours
          Monthly-Vacation-Hours
          Monthly-Sick-Hours
          Monthly-Holiday-Hours
        Monthly-Withholding-Amount
        Federal-Tax-Amount
         Monthly-Gross-Pay
         Federal-Tax-Rate
          Tax-Status
          Number-of-Exemptions

Figure 15: Continued

State-Tax-Amount
Monthly Gross-Pay
State-Tax-Rate
Tax-Status
State-of-Residence
State-of-Employment
Number-of-Exemptions
Monthly-Deduction-Amount
Life-Insurance-Amount
Medical-Insurance-Amount
Type-of-Coverage
Coverage-Rate
Monthly-Accruals
Vacation-Hours
Vacation-Rate
Employment-Classification
Years-of-Employment
Date-of-Hire
Current-Pay-Period-Date
Sick-Leave-Hours
Sick-Leave-Rate
Employment-Classification
Years-of-Employment
Date-of-Hire
Current-Pay-Period-Date

Figure 15: Continued

Step 3: Define Data Relationships

Method: For each raw input data item, specify what other data items are required to determine its value, and organize the data items into groups such that all members of a group have a common key.

The set of data items necessary to determine a single value for a particular data item is referred to as its *key*. For example, social-security-number will determine a single value for employee-name;

customer-number will determine a single value for customer-name. More than one data item may be necessary to determine a single value; for example, a single value for employee-quarter-to-date-gross-pay is determined by both a social-security-number and a quarter-number. Social-security-number will be a sufficient key for many data items in an employee data base. For example, an employee cannot have more than one date-of-birth or one sex, but he or she may certainly have had more than one previous employer and more than one degree. Employment-start-date or employment-end-date is necessary to determine a single value for previous-employer-name. Year-of-degree and type-of-degree are necessary to determine a single value for major-subject and school-name.

Data items should be grouped together by their keys—that is, those items that have the same keys should be placed in the same group. Some of the raw input data items listed in Figure 15 are grouped by their keys in Figure 16.

The interface system is summarized in Figure 17.

Step 4: Define Computer Outputs

Define the set of computer outputs that satisfy the information needs developed in step 1. For those in which the content and form can be predefined, prepare prototypes of a page, screen, or other appropriate unit. The content should be defined in terms of data items, and the format should include the desired sequence in which the data is to be presented. For each output, list all other requirements, such as frequency, schedule, means of distribution, and security measures. Useful dimensions for organizing the outputs are:

1. type of data content (customer detail, department summary);
2. type of data receiver (employees, customers, managers, board members);
3. production schedule (daily, weekly, monthly, annually);
4. response-time requirements (within 10 seconds, 2 hours, 1 day).

For outputs that are to be produced on a *predefined schedule*, the requirements should be expressed in terms of frequency and deadline, such as daily by noon, weekly by Tuesday morning, or

Keys:	Data Items:
Social-Security-Number	Employee-Name Employee-Sex Employee-Date-of-Birth Employee-Date-of-Hire Employment-Classification Employee-Department-Number Hourly-Rate Tax-Status Number-of-Exemptions State-of-Residence State-of-Employment
Social-Security-Number + Month-Number	Monthly-Regular-Hours Monthly-Overtime-Hours Monthly-Vacation-Hours Monthly-Sick-Hours Monthly-Holiday-Hours Monthly-Withholding-Amount
Social-Security-Number + Year-of-Degree + Type-of-Degree	Major-Subject School-Name
Social-Security-Number + Previous-Employment-Start- Date	Previous-Employment-End-Date Previous-Employer-Name Previous-Employment-Title Previous-Employment-Ending- Salary
State-of-Residence + Tax-Status + Number-of-Exemptions	State-Tax-Rate
Employment-Classification + Years-of-Employment	Vacation-Rate Sick-Leave-Rate

Figure 16: Grouping data items by keys

Inputs: **Outputs:**

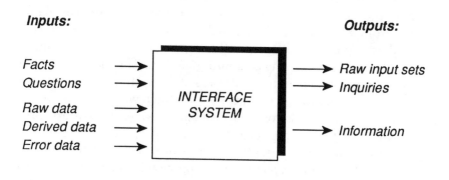

Figure 17: Interface system model

monthly by the third working day of the month. It may be appropriate to specify the scheduling requirement in relation to another event, such as within two working days after monthly closing of accounts or within three hours after the last input data is received.

For outputs that are to be produced on *request*, specify the response-time requirements in terms of elapsed time between the request and the generation of output. If both maximum and average response times are important, state both as requirements. For example, five minutes may be an acceptable worst case, but an average of less than two minutes may be critical for efficient operations.

Step 5: Define Inquiry Capabilities

For those outputs that are to be available on request, determine what is needed to support the end users making the requests for output. Specify response-time requirements for validating the requests and for producing the requested output. Outputs needed within, say, ten minutes or less, will generally require an on-line request process. If the volume of output and the form in which it is to be presented are amenable to terminal display, then the output may be produced on-line as well.

To determine the method appropriate for requesting output reports, you will need to consider the type of end user (casual or experienced) and the type of requests (predefined reports or the ability to create new reports). When the report content and format are predefined, the simplest approach is often to present a *menu* of available reports from which the end user makes a choice by typing the corresponding report number or positioning the screen pointer (cursor) at the selection and pressing an appropriate key. The menu approach is especially helpful for infrequent users of the system. Directions for its use can be displayed on the screen along with the menu. In addition, the user's password can determine which menus are presented. The major disadvantage to the menu approach is that the report format and data contents generally must be predefined.

When the inquiry capability must provide a way for the user to supply additional parameter data, such as which customers are to be included in the report or in what sequence the report should be presented, the interface is more complex. For these types of inquiries, the requirements should address the type and level of computer assistance to support the request process. Two standard approaches are the use of a command language or the development of a question and answer dialog to solicit the parameters from the user.

The first method is usually called *command mode* and the latter is frequently referred to as *conversation mode*. The use of conversation mode provides more flexibility than menu mode; however, it may still be limited since the questions included in the dialog will be the only ones asked. The drawback to the use of a command language is that it is often confusing to casual users who need more than minimal prompting. Refer to Chapter 8, Human-Friendly Interfaces, for additional discussion of this topic.

Step 6: Identify Sources of Inputs

Method: Determine the source for each raw input data item identified in Step 2. Where and in what form does each exist in the external system? What other data items refer to the same subject and originate in the same place and at the same time?

Group together those data items that have a common source, frequency, and timing of data collection, and those that relate to the same subject, such as customer, employee, or product. These *input*

Transaction	Input Data Items
Employee Application Form	Social-Security-Number Employee-Name Employee-Sex Employee-Date-of-Birth State-of-Residence Year-of-Degree Type-of-Degree School-Name Major-Subject Previous-Employment-Start-Date Previous-Employment-End-Date Previous-Employer-Name Previous-Employment-Title Previous-Employment-Ending-Salary
Employee Hiring Form	Employee-Date-of-Hire Employment-Classification State-of-Employment Employee-Department-Number Hourly-Rate Tax-Status Number-of-Exemptions

Figure 18: Sample input transactions

sets, or *transactions*, are entered into the computer system. Some of the data items from Figure 16 are shown in Figure 18 grouped logically into transactions.

The raw input data items should be organized into input sets that can be conveniently collected and entered into the computer. Data items that are produced at the same time, by the same source, are logical candidates for forming an input set. Those that refer to the same subject (that is, have the same key) are also candidates for placement in the same group, since they may be collected together

Transaction Specification	Example
Frequency	Daily
Volume	30 per day
Response time for error detection feedback	1 second
Maximum time for changes to reach files	1 hour
External form	Handwritten paper document
Data item contents and order of entry	List of each data item on the form

Figure 19: Transaction specifications

and their key would only need to be entered once for the entire transaction.

If data collection is a manual process, a transaction is often analogous to a source document or form, such as an employment application form. If data collection is an automated process, perhaps data generated by another computer system, a transaction is often a record on a file.

For each transaction type, specify the information shown in Figure 19:

Step 7: Define Data-Entry Procedures

Method: Using the information gathered in Step 6, determine the appropriate methods to use for the data-entry interface.

For on-line data entry, it is often desirable to display a screen format that resembles the input form as closely as possible. You should therefore include with your specifications a sample of a source document, if one exists, or prepare a prototype of the form or an appropriate screen display.

Volume and frequency estimates are used in the design phase to determine what type of internal process is most efficient for data storage and retrieval. The combination of volume and frequency often provides the best description of input patterns. For example, although an employee may change his or her address at any time, the personnel department may choose to make address updates once a week. Your experience can indicate how many address changes are received during an average week. Volumes also may vary at different frequencies. Take the example of salary changes. On a weekly basis, less than 1 percent of employee salaries may change. On the other hand, once a year, when annual salary adjustments are made, 100 percent may change. It may be desirable to develop a different procedure for handling the annual salary adjustments because the volume is so much greater.

The volume and frequency estimates should be realistic and should cover current and anticipated future requirements, because this information is used to determine efficient access to stored data, required storage capacity, speed of data storage devices, and the appropriate level of data-entry interface. Future requirements should be stated as percent change expected—for example, number-of employees may increase by 10 percent per year. Overstating the volume requirements is likely to increase computer costs. For example, larger than necessary disk storage units may be purchased. Understating the requirements may result in an inadequate system based on several causes. The storage capacity may be inadequate, the processing speed may be too slow to handle the number of terminal users and input volume of each user, and the data-entry interface may be inappropriate for high-volume data entry.

The data collection method must be determined for each input set, or transaction type. Specify the procedure from the source of the data (point of origin) to the point of entry into the computer. For transactions that require on-line data entry, decide on the desirable level of computer assistance for this task. The conversational mode, which solicits the input data by a series of *prompts*, or questions, requires minimal familiarity with the system on the part of the end user, since a direct prompt such as *enter customer number*, can appear for each data item. However, this approach can waste time and prove frustrating for the experienced user, who must wait for each prompt before entering the next data item. It is also not suitable for high-volume data entry. Use it for transactions in which frequency and volume of use are low, and which casual users are most likely to be entering.

For high-volume data entry, other approaches should be considered, such as that of displaying column headings for data items to be entered and permitting many transactions to be entered on a screen. To use this approach, decide what level of error detection feedback is required and how often it should be displayed—every data item, every transaction, every ten transactions, each screen, for instance.

The final specification related to data entry is the data correction process. How will input errors detected by the computer be resolved and reentered? If error feedback is provided on-line at the time of input, the correction procedure may be simple. If the input data is not subject to complete validation at the time of data entry, or if the data conversion is done off-line, a more complex correction procedure

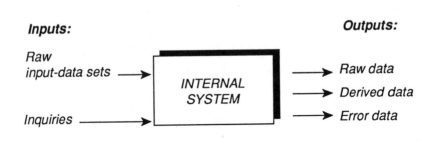

Inputs: **Outputs:**

Raw
input-data sets ──────▶ INTERNAL SYSTEM ──────▶ Raw data
                                          ──────▶ Derived data
Inquiries ──────────▶   ──────▶ Error data

Figure 20: Internal system model

may be required. How do the errors get related back to a source document? How are the original source documents stored for efficient access to resolve data-entry errors?

Internal system tasks are shown in Figure 20.

Step 8: Specify Data Validation Procedures

The adage "Garbage in, garbage out" applies to all systems, including computers. Since all outputs ultimately derive from the *raw* inputs entered into the system, computer outputs can never be more correct than the inputs on which they are based. A system that is highly interactive, easy to use, and highly responsive is worth little if the outputs cannot be relied upon for correctness. Time invested in carefully specifying all the validation procedures will pay off in correctness of outputs and, therefore, in subsequent end-user acceptance and confidence in the system.

Data validation can be viewed as having three levels:

1. absolute checking of a data item against its permissible range of possible values;
2. consistency checking of a data item with other data items within the same transaction;
3. consistency checking of a data item with other data items previously stored on the data base.

The first level of data validation is often done as a part of an on-line data entry interface, for example, checking an employee salary against a range of permissible salaries.

Step 9: Define Data Protection Requirements

Method: Determine the level of data protection required for the system.

Data protection must be considered from such perspectives as protection against unauthorized access to the data base, protection against accidental destruction of data, and ability to recover from loss of data and computing facilities. The costs associated with data protection can be high; therefore, this is an area in which careful cost-benefit analysis should receive top priority.

The information stored in the computer can be extremely valuable to your organization; in fact, the organization may not be able to function effectively without it. To protect this valuable resource, measures should be taken to create *backup copies* of the data base at reasonable time intervals. What reasonable intervals are depends on how critical the data is, how often and how extensively the data is updated, and how much it would cost to recreate the data lost since the last backup copy was made. In addition, these calculations should consider the lost business opportunity costs created by the data loss. Creating backup copies of the data base at periodic intervals and building a copy of all transactions as they are processed between data base backup creation can provide a measure of protection against the toll exacted by hardware or software failures.

In the event of a disaster such as a fire or flood, these backup files are likely to be destroyed as well unless they are stored at a different location. Yet if the computing facilities are damaged, the fact that the files are retrievable from another site may not provide immediate recovery abilities. The application system will be inoperative until the computing facilities are restored or until an alternative computing site can be found. If the application is extremely critical to the business even during a disaster recovery period, then such arrangements should be made in advance and periodically revalidated for feasibility. The importance of an on-line reservation system is so critical to airlines, for example, that they acquire redundant hardware to cover situations in which a hardware malfunction would make the system inoperative. Some organizations make reciprocal arrangements with other computing centers to provide facilities in the event that either becomes inoperative for a period of time. Commercial time-sharing services also offer disaster recovery facilities for fixed monthly fees, somewhat like accident insurance. It is also possible to purchase insurance that provides financial compensation during the recovery period. If the income side of the business would suffer greatly during such a period and if the additional expenses incurred were significant (such as hiring temporary staff to operate the system manually), then disaster insurance might be appropriate.

Data security, or protection against unauthorized access to the data base and application software, involves different considerations. How sensitive, proprietary, or confidential is the data? Some kinds of data, such as payroll, may be internally sensitive; others—product design data, for example—may be externally sensitive. The typical commercially available operating systems provide very little real access security other than a system of passwords that control access to software programs and data bases. Some terminals offer such additional security mechanisms as a key or magnetic card that must be inserted before the terminal will operate.

If the application data is externally sensitive and organizationally valuable, and if the computing facility supports remote dial-up capabilities, additional security precautions should be investigated. One alternative is to store the data in an encrypted form. Encryption will increase the operational cost of the system and may result in longer response times, but these may be justified by the gain in data security.

In the normal course of operating the application system, different levels of security may be appropriate. For example, while many data items on an employee data base may be updated by any of the staff in the personnel department, perhaps extra authorization in the form of a password known only to a few persons should be required to change a salary by more than 10 percent. In the sales management system, all staff members may be allowed to display summary reports of quarterly sales by product type, but only the sales manager may display reports containing sales data for individual salespersons. In a budget management system, a department manager may be allowed to display employee salaries for the persons within that department, but not for employees in other departments.

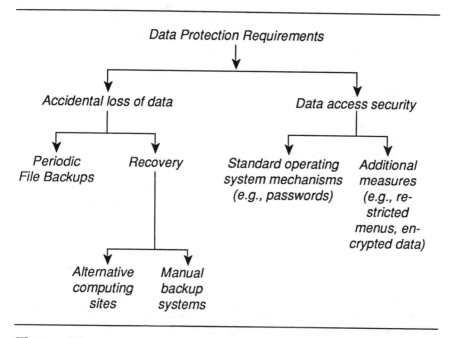

Figure 21: Data protection requirements

Figure 21 shows a structure for defining requirements for data protection.

Step 10: Specify Data Derivation Rules

Method: Specify the functional methods, formulae, mappings, and so forth, for producing each of the derived data items.

The derivations should be communicated through an unambiguous statement of the rules to be used. These rules may take many forms, the most common being a formula such as:

Gross-Pay = Hourly-Rate × (Hours-Worked + Sick Leave-Hours
+ Vacation-Hours + Holiday-Hours)

Other derivations may involve establishing a data item based on ranges of values of another data item, such as:

Insurance-Age-Code = 1 if Age less than 20,
2 if Age > or = 20 and < 30,
3 if Age > or = 30 and < 40,
4 if Age > or = 40

Some derivations may involve meeting certain criteria among several data items, such as:

Customer-
Discount-Rate = 10 if year-to-date-sales   > $10,000 or

last-order-amount   > $1,000

Customer-
Discount-Rate = 05 if year-to-date-sales   > $5,000 or

last-order-amount   >$1,000

Customer-
Discount-Rate = 00 if year-to-date-sales   < or =

$5,000 and last-order-amount

< or = $1,000

Other derivations may require a table of possible input values each with an associated derived value, like the one below used to derive a state-name from a state-code:

State Code:	*State Name:*
CO	Colorado
FL	Florida
MA	Massachusetts
TN	Tennessee

The formulae involved in frequently used derivations, such as sum, average, and percent, are obvious, but exercise careful judgment about just what derivations are self-evident. Ambrose Bierce supplied an apt definition for the term self-evident: "Evident to one's self and to nobody else."

Supply the derivation rules in a form that is convenient for clear and unambiguous communication to the software developers.

Chapter 6

THE CONTINUING ROLE OF THE USER

COMPUTER DESIGN REVIEW

After the user has prepared a requirements definition, the software developers use it as the basis of their systems design and cost estimate. The systems design may include several alternatives, perhaps at varying cost levels. During the design phase, the user should remain available to answer any questions that may arise or to clarify any points in the requirements specification. The user may also need to make some preliminary decisions during the design phase if conflicts in function and cost parameters become apparent.

The design proposals presented to the user should not be filled with computer jargon. With a well-structured requirements specification in hand, the designers should be able to relate their proposal to it and present their design using a similar structure and terminology. Any areas of the design that do not seem directly relatable to the specifications should be questioned by the user.

The costs for features specified as optional by the user for both development and operational components should accompany the design. The user can then compare these costs with the marginal benefits of the optional features and decide whether or not these features should be included.

Decisions made during this review process may necessitate further design work and subsequent design reviews. The process should be viewed as an iterative one. As decisions are made such as which of the optional features are to be included, which are to be deferred for a follow-up project, and which are rejected, the requirements definition should be amended to reflect them. The requirements definition should be brought up to date with information that will provide a record of the basis on which decisions were made. Circumstances may change in the future, thus altering the cost-benefit ratio. For example, an optional feature rejected at first because its hardware costs were too high may now be acceptable because costs have since come down.

If the developers take a top-down approach to systems design, the user can be involved at many stages during the design phase. The design reviews can be conducted for different aspects of the system, such as data base design, interface system design, and internal system design. If the developers have access to state-of-the-art application development tools, the design review process can include demonstrations of prototypes of the system. Such demonstrations provide a basis for good communication and user feedback, and are generally far more meaningful than verbal descriptions, flowcharts, and other methods of describing what the system will be like. Chapter 7 discusses various methods of top-down implementation that permit the user to stay on top of what is happening during the design and development process.

EXTERNAL PROCEDURE DESIGN

The user is primarily responsible for the detailed design and implementation of the manual procedures that occur outside the computer system. These procedures usually fall into the areas of data collection and dissemination of outputs. Source forms may need to be designed and printed, and training or instruction in their use may be required. Procedures may need to be developed and documented. Supplies and furniture (such as terminal tables) may be needed. Office space may require renovation or rewiring to accommodate terminals and other equipment that will be used in the new system. To the extent that these areas relate to the external system, the user should be responsible for their implementation.

Much of this external procedure design and implementation work can be done parallel with the computer software development. Coordination will be required between the two efforts so that subsequent changes in one do not invalidate the other. As the software development work progresses, more of these ancillary decisions can be made and implemented. Decisions that are dependent on the finer details of the software should not be made prematurely.

The distinction between external system processes and the external components of the interface system is sometimes difficult to discern. Rather than relegate important areas to chance, establish a clear understanding of the respective responsibilities of the user and the developer. Make certain that each group is aware of what tasks the other group is managing. Inadvertently, the user and the developer may duplicate each other's efforts in these areas.

ACCEPTANCE TESTING

In preparation for the evaluation phase, the user should begin developing an acceptance-test procedure. This work should be done during the software development phase so that the test and the software are ready at the same time.

Acceptance tests frequently involve either creating *test* data to enter into the system or developing a set of *live* data from several cycles or time periods. When a current system exists, either manual or automated, the live data can be run through both the current system and the new system so that the outputs from both can be compared. This is called a *parallel system test*. Although this test is often useful, it can be frustrating and unmanageable when the old system does not produce correct outputs. Much time can be wasted trying to understand why the old system did not produce the same answer as the new one.

In addition to testing the system for its functional ability to receive inputs, detect input errors, and produce the desired outputs, measures should be developed for testing other requirements, such as response times, security, and meeting deadlines. If live data is supplied, it may need to be supplemented by test data in order to evaluate unusual conditions and pathological cases.

The acceptance test may be exercised many times. For those parts of the software that fail, revisions can be made and the test rerun. An important point to remember is that this is a user-acceptance test of the *system*, and not of the competence of the system developers. It makes no sense for the user to make a secret of what the test includes. First, the predefined measurable objectives established in the design specifications should form the basis of the test. Since these are already published, the testing should not include any surprises. To reveal additional requirements at the testing stage is capricious, and whether or not they are met is a matter of chance. Legitimate requirements should not be left to chance; they must be included in the specifications. Second, if the tests are indeed based on the original requirements and are therefore predictable and defensible, why keep them a secret? The developers will have to waste their energies devising their own tests unless the user's tests are available to them during the software development phase. If the tests are comprehensive and each result is objectively measurable, then the system either meets all the requirements or it fails to meet some of them. It makes no difference that the developers knew what was included in the test; the system either passes or fails. Third, since the system, rather than the developers, is being tested, the developers may participate in preparing a comprehensive system testing procedure. Developers become intimately familiar with their code and can provide insight into unusual conditions that should be incorporated in the testing procedure. I strongly recommend that the development of tests be a joint effort, but with the user assuming primary responsibility for ensuring their completeness—that is, that every important requirement is measured by the acceptance testing procedure.

Not only should the software be tested, so should the documentation. At least one person, preferably a potential end user, should exercise all the system components using the documentation and training materials, including on-line help facilities if provided. Discrepancies between the system's behavior and its documentation should be resolved before the system is in use. Users of new systems are not only frustrated by incorrect documentation, they can lose confidence in the system itself.

SYSTEM EVALUATION

> [That] the wisdom of an act is judged by the outcome, the result . . . is immortal nonsense; the wisdom of an act is to be judged by the light that the doer had when he performed it.
>
> —Ambrose Bierce,
> *The Devil's Dictionary*

The system must be evaluated on the basis of the goals, objectives, and requirements communicated in the system specifications.

Analysis of the test results is the basis of the system evaluation. Some measures may be pass or fail, while others may be matters of degree. You may decide that while the criteria for some tests are not yet met, the system is performing well enough to be put into operation. In this case, you can *provisionally accept* the system for use while the required revisions are being made. Although this is a typical situation, make clear which requirements remain to be met before the system will be fully acceptable. After each acceptance test note the deficiencies, and once the developers revise the system reapply the tests.

When the system meets all the conditions of the acceptance test, future enhancements and desirable revisions can be considered. These suggestions should be included in a *postimplementation report,* together with suggestions generated during an initial period of system use in real operation. Such a report can form the basis of a requirements definition for a follow-up project in the future. Too often, however, one is never prepared. Any project, however well done, could probably have been better done, and when this type of information is lost, we have lessened our ability to learn from our mistakes and to pass on some valuable experiences to others.

Part Three

HOW TO CONTROL THE END RESULTS

Nothing ... will ever be attempted, if all possible objections must first be overcome.

—Samuel Johnson,
Rasselas

Chapter 7

MANAGEMENT STRATEGIES

ORGANIZATIONAL STRUCTURES AND THEIR EFFECTS

If you are the manager of the application area to be supported by the computer system, I recommend that you assume professional responsibility for developing the requirements definition and do as much as possible of the systems analysis yourself. For large systems, you will certainly need to delegate some of the work to members of your staff, and there are good reasons for doing so. They get involved in the system early and feel that they have had an influence on it; you get the benefit of perspectives different from your own.

If the scope of the application is greater than that of your authority within the organization, or if other organizational circumstances demand that you not take full responsibility for preparing the requirements definition, you might choose to involve a *review committee*. Such a committee functions in a review and approval role, so do not expect it to do any of the analysis tasks required to prepare a comprehensive design specification. Such tasks cannot be done by committee in any case. Although the use of a committee may lessen your personal risk, you will have placed important decisions at the whim of individual members, who may have little in-depth knowledge of the real application needs. It also appears to be a universal law that anything done by committee will take longer, since meeting times must be coordinated, the subjects must be explained to each member's satisfaction, and some members will find the meetings a convenient forum to serve their own ends.

You should carefully weigh the pros and cons of the review committee approach before pursuing it. Use it only as a last resort when, because of the organizational climate, you simply cannot accept

89

the level of personal risk involved in taking sole responsibility for the design specifications, or you are not allowed to. If a design committee is used, be aware that its system design specifications will usually reflect the compromises, inconsistencies, and lack of coherent perspectives of its members.

Another approach, which allows broad participation across organizational lines, is the *project team*. This strategy can often be used to address organizational concerns without the disadvantages of review committees.

If you use this approach, select people with relevant expertise, rather than organizational status, as members of the project team. The team members work on parts of the design specification where their experience is applicable. The products of their efforts are submitted to you, as the project manager, for review, approval, and integration of the individual parts into a coherent whole. Using this strategy, you retain control of and responsibility for the design specification, and you, rather than a committee, make the final decisions. You may choose to run the project teams as democratically as you wish. Topics may be placed before the team for discussion and recommendations, and perhaps even a vote if you feel comfortable doing so. The people selected for the team should understand that they are assigned specific work to do and are not in a role of approving your decisions. Problems encountered with the project team approach are the typical ones of overlay management that occur when a person who officially reports to someone else in the hierarchy is given an assignment that involves reporting to a different project manager for a portion of her or his time. Difficult problems are rarely encountered unless the managers involved disagree on relevant issues.

I recommend this strategy is you have sufficient management experience and can provide strong leadership for the team. You must also be willing to take responsibility for the project and the end results. By having several people working on different parts of the system at the same time, the project can be completed sooner. And if all members of the team are using similar analysis techniques, then their individual efforts can be integrated more easily. You should set up some standards or guidelines for the team to follow and communicate your expectations clearly with regard to the form and content of what they will be submitting to you.

With this approach you benefit from a broader base of expertise, and more individuals are familiar with the design specifications. If the team members are potential end users, their early involvement and influence will give them a sense of ownership of the final system. They can become your best ambassadors among their peers for selling the ideas incorporated in the system. Be aware that a well-designed and well-implemented system can still fail if no one uses it effectively. Thus you must consider the psychological preparedness of your staff for the use of computers. If, because of a lack of prior positive computer exposure, they see the advent of automation as threatening, their recalcitrance toward learning and using the system effectively can be exhibited in subtle ways. Often, however, the enthusiasm and confidence expressed by their peers during the development project will allay some of their concerns.

MEASURING PROGRESS DURING SOFTWARE DEVELOPMENT

This section discusses user involvement in the later phases of system development: system design, implementation, and evaluation. My assumption is that the user will want to continue to control the end results even after the requirements are specified, and will do everything possible to continue to improve the products of each phase.

Part 2 of this book presented a top-down methodology for systems analysis. This section will discuss several top-down approaches to system design and implementation, which computer staffs are adopting in ever-increasing numbers. In contrast to a top-down approach, a bottom-up approach is one in which the most detailed parts of the system are designed and programmed first, and then all components of the system are combined, sometimes fitting together only by brute force. A major disadvantage to this approach is that no one knows until the end whether all the pieces will fit together and whether the end is even close, because the pieces do not work as a system until all are complete and integrated. Historically, computer systems were developed in this manner, and it is no small wonder that neither users nor developers had much control over final results, schedules, or development costs. Fortunately, as the software development industry matured, numerous case studies revealed that the characteristics of successful computer projects seemed to center around top-down design and implementation strategies. These strategies are embodied in methodologies such as *composite design* and *structured programming*. All of these techniques can be used together to develop more reliable software in more cost-effective ways.

Software consists of program modules, which are units of software designed to perform a single predefined function. *Top-down implementation* simply means that given a set of hierarchical program functions, the design of the program modules is done from the top down. The coding and testing of the modules is also done in this manner.

In the system layer model presented in Part 1 of this book, the top layer of the computer system is the interface system. If top-down design and implementation approaches are used, then the interface components of the system will be the first to be developed. This portion of the system can be demonstrated to the users early and realistic feedback can be given to the developers. Flowcharts and other diagrams are abstract representations of the real system, therefore it is often difficult to determine from them how the system will really work. Early working versions of portions of the system provide real examples of the direction of the end product.

Example is always more efficacious than precept.
—Samuel Johnson,
Rasselas

The advantages of the top-down approach to design and implementation address four major areas of concern.

1. *Improved quality of the final system software:*
   a. reveals the major interface problems early in the development process.

Since the major interfaces among program modules are resolved first, any significant system design flaws will be discovered early. Furthermore, as the development project nears its end, the remaining program interface problems to be resolved will be the minor ones, since they are by definition the smallest modules at the bottom of the hierarchy. Their scope of effect is narrow and well-defined, and thus one small problem will not upset the whole system and necessitate substantial redesign.

    b. allows function to identify the data items that are required by each program module.

A measure of system reliability is how well the integrity of the data base is maintained while adding, changing, and removing data items within it. One approach to maintaining data base integrity is to restrict its vulnerability by permitting each program module access to the most minimal set of data items necessary to perform its function. If testing reveals erroneous data in the system, the search for the corrupt module is limited to the smallest possible set. Also, a module in which every condition has not been thoroughly tested will, at least, have the smallest possible adverse effect on the data base.

    c. minimizes retrofitting.

Because the system is developing from the top down, the consequences of a new requirement can be traced from the top down to the affected modules, which can then be redesigned in view of the new requirement. The bottom-up alternative results in retrofits—that is, patch-ups to the modules to add functions that were not part of their original design.

    2. *More efficient use of development resources:*
        a. spreads hardware requirements more evenly over the entire development process.

Often, the computer on which development work is done is also used for other production work. Few organizations have the luxury of unlimited computer time to devote to development projects, and to the extent that competition exists for limited resources within the development project, spreading the required computing resources over the longest period of the development cycle is desirable. Bottom-up approaches relegate the bulk of program and system testing to the end of the cycle, placing a high demand for computer resources in a short time span; in contrast, few computing resources are used in the early phases.

      b. boosts morale because tangible results are seen early in the development process.

With bottom-up approaches, operation of the overall system cannot be seen until every piece is completed and all are working effectively together. With the top-down approach, the top-level interfaces are developed first and can be demonstrated even though the detailed functions are yet to be developed. Both users and developers can see the system evolve as each next level of functions is added. These demonstrations are possible through the use of *dummy stubs*, which are simple modules that temporarily substitute for those modules yet to be developed at the next lower levels of the program module hierarchy. For example, the user interface for the sales management system can be demonstrated before many of the lower-level functions are developed. Users can work with the order entry screens prior to the development of a module that determines the prices for the products ordered if the system simply contains a dummy stub for that function, such as one that always produces $100 as the price for any product ordered. The lack of a real module to perform this function does not affect the testing of the appropriateness of the screen displays and user interaction within the order processing system.

    3. *Improved user and developer communications:*
        a. provides a working demonstration system early in the process, and therefore involves the user more realistically in the development process.

The user reviews a tangible, working skeletal system early in the development cycle, rather than abstract paper models such as flowcharts. Reviewing the real system interfaces solicits feedback based on user expertise rather than the cursory feedback often associated with the review of progress reports and design charts.

    b. provides meaningful user feedback throughout the development process.

The system can be demonstrated to the user as each new function is added. The user does not have to speculate or imagine how the system will work in a real operational environment. With continual and meaningful feedback, potential misunderstandings are avoided, the costs of misdirection are minimized, and potential improvements can be quickly incorporated and evaluated.

    c. shows continual progress as the system evolves.

The user can see the results of the development efforts throughout the cycle rather than waiting until the end. Since the user is likely to be paying directly or indirectly for the system, positive and continual indications of how the resources are being used are valuable. Actually seeing the system develop is more meaningful than viewing PERT charts and budget figures. Developers can spend more time building the system if they are relieved of writing frequent reports on what they are doing.

    4. *Lower development and operational costs:*
        a. allows incremental integration testing and error correction.

Designing a full integration test for a large system can be a formidable task. However, if the system is built one module at a time then test procedures can also be developed as each module is built. Each new test procedure can be added to the previous test suite. Each new version of the test suite provides a full test of the currently completed modules. If new errors are detected, the likely culprit is the last module added or a module that interfaces with it. Testing in this way is not only more cost and time efficient, it is also likely to be more thorough. Writing small *dummy stubs* to substitute temporarily for functions yet to be programmed is far easier, and therefore less costly, than writing complex programs to serve as *test drivers* for the many small unrelated modules developed early in the bottom-up approach.

    b. increases productivity by spreading the use of computing resources more evenly over the development cycle, as discussed earlier.

    c. reduces costs associated with redesign and reprogramming by encouraging earlier and more meaningful user feedback.

    d. produces software that is more thoroughly tested and more accurately targeted on user needs.

Such software will have lower overall development, operational, and maintenance costs.

There are three categories of top-down approach available. The *radical* top-down approach is one in which the top-level module is both designed and implemented before any lower-level modules are even considered. Each successive level is then designed and implemented before the next and so on. The *conservative* top-down approach separates the design phase from the implementation phase and designs all modules, starting at the top level, before coding and testing any of them. After all modules are designed, coding and testing begin, again starting at the top. Between these two extremes is the *look-ahead* top-down approach, in which several levels at one time are designed, and then coded and tested.

Each of these approaches has its pros and cons. The choice depends on the characteristics of the application. This section describes the advantages and disadvantages of each one.

> **Radical top-down approach:** Design and code each module, starting at the top, before designing the next lower-level modules.

Advantages:

1. Provides the earliest possible working demonstration system for the user and is most appropriate when user requirements are not well defined. The user may then see the results of

each level of the specification before further work proceeds, thereby allowing continuing refinement of user requirements.

2. If time pressures, rather than budget, are the most severe constraint, then this strategy ensures that the most implementation is done before the deadline is reached. If the project is subject to premature termination for a missed deadline, this strategy maximizes evidence of progress which may help justify extensions; if not, at least a partial system may be implemented.

Disadvantages:

1. Since the coding of each module immediately follows its design, the temptation to code prematurely, in advance of adequate design work, may lead to later requirements being retrofitted. This may have an adverse affect on the quality of the final software, since retrofitted programs are performing functions in ways for which they were not originally designed.

2. If subsequent problems with the design are encountered at lower levels, then the earlier coding efforts may have to be redone, which may contribute to increased development costs.

Conservative top-down approach: Design all modules, starting at the top, before coding and testing any of them.

Advantages:

1. If the foremost objective is developing the highest quality software as opposed to minimizing development time and costs, this approach is appropriate since all design is done first and the entire design is known before any of the coding begins. This approach eliminates the temptation to begin coding without adequate design, and therefore reduces the possibility of having to retrofit unanticipated requirements to already developed software modules.

2. If accurate estimates are essential at the beginning of each phase of the system development project, they are much easier to produce if the entire system is designed first. Estimating development costs for a completely designed system is more reliable than estimating on the basis of a partial design or requirements specification.

Disadvantages:

1. Knowing all specifications and requirements in order to design a system completely, before any implementation and the feedback that demonstrations provide, is difficult. Often, users will get much clearer ideas of what they want the system to do as they see parts of the system working. To the extent that the requirements are likely to change after the design is complete, some of the advantages of this approach are lost. It is best applied to systems that can be well defined in advance and that are not treading on entirely new ground.

2. Since all design work is done first, the working demonstration is not available until the design is complete and the top-level module is coded. The users do not see progress as early as with the *radical* approach, since a working demonstration is not available until the top-level module is coded, and therefore they are not as meaningfully involved during the design phase.

Look-ahead top-down approach: Design several levels from the top down before coding and testing modules.

Advantages:

1. If the project has conflicting requirements, such as minimizing costs and maximizing software quality, then this hybrid approach will come closest to achieving both.

2. The disadvantages of both the radical and conservative approaches are reduced: less redesign is necessary when new requirements are discovered than with the radical approach, and the working demonstration is available sooner than with the conservative approach.

The three approaches are illustrated in Figure 23 using a simple system, consisting of three program modules labeled A, B, and C, to produce the financial statement shown in Figure 22.

For illustration purposes, let us assume that it takes one day each to design, code, and test each of the program modules. Further, we will assume that the testing includes demonstrations for end users. Figure 23 provides a comparison among the three types of top-down implementation showing what activities will take place on each day.

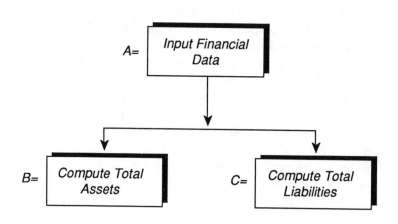

Figure 22: Sample system to produce a financial statement

	Radical	Look-Ahead	Conservative
Day 1:	Design A	Design A	Design A
Day 2:	Code A	Design B	Design B
Day 3:	**Demo A**	Code A	Design C
Day 4:	Design B	**Demo A**	Code A
Day 5:	Code B	Design C	**Demo A**
Day 6:	Demo A & B	Code B	Code B
Day 7:	Design C	Demo A & B	Demo A & B
Day 8:	Code C	Code C	Code C
Day 9:	Demo A & B & C	Demo A & B & C	Demo A & B & C

Figure 23: Comparisons of top-down approaches

Figure 23 shows the earliest time at which a demonstration of the user interface portion of the system is available, assuming each task takes one day to complete. The redesign loop is indicated by the arrows which show how much work will need to be redone if the first demonstration results in necessary revisions. For the radical approach, three days' work would be affected. For the look-ahead approach, four days' work, and for the conservative, five days' work may need to be redone. However, the conservative and look-ahead approaches do permit earlier redesign in case problems are encountered in the design for A when the design for B is attempted. In this case, only one day's work is affected versus three days' work with the radical approach.

Chapter 8

SUPPORT FOR A USABLE SYSTEM

INTEGRATED DOCUMENTATION

Documentation is important, particularly for the long-term viability and adaptability of the system. Users should be sensitive to the real needs for documentation and know how to ensure its production. Although much lip service is paid to the importance of adequate documentation, it is rarely provided, and still more rarely used. Commonly, the documentation is relegated to the end of the development cycle, by which time budgets and schedules have often been exceeded, and the documentation effort is thus forgone or hastily prepared. The developers rarely object, since the task is usually tedious and often thankless. Nevertheless, there are some guidelines the user can follow to obtain useful documentation.

1. Establish clearly defined objectives for each type of documentation you require. State the purpose and audience for each one.
2. Make the production of all types of documentation an integral part of the development process. Do not allow it to be left to the end of the cycle.
3. Establish measurement criteria for the documentation and include the testing of its accuracy and appropriateness as part of the acceptance testing procedures.
4. Be practical and goal directed about the documentation you require. Demanding elaborate documentation simply as a means of controlling the project is wasteful of resources and may be done at the expense of your real needs.

The top-down implementation approach facilitates the integration of documentation tasks with the design and coding tasks by permitting each function to be documented as it is developed and tested. Developers who produce documentation in small quantities throughout the cycle are more likely to document accurately and thoroughly, since they are recording information while it is fresh in their minds. The task is less onerous when done in small increments.

Required documentation falls into three basic categories:

1. a record of how the system was developed;
2. information on how the system is operated;
3. technical documentation on how the system can be maintained, such as how it is internally structured and how to incorporate future requirements and revisions.

Both the audience for and the purpose of each type of documentation are different. The next several sections discuss these properties for each type.

System Development

The audience for documentation on how the system was developed is primarily managerial, in that the purpose is to record why various design and implementation decisions were made. Documentation relating to actual costs for various system components and project phases versus their budgeted costs would fall into this category, as would schedule estimates versus actual time and effort expended. This documentation should include the requirements definition, the results of cost-benefit analyses, and any alternative design proposals together with the reasons for their rejection.

The purpose of system development documentation is to provide an historical documentation record that may lead to improvements in project management abilities. This documentation may be used in several ways:

1. It may be useful for estimating future development projects.
2. It may be useful for evaluating future suggestions for revisions

to the application system, especially if the rationales for the previous development decisions are included.

3. It may be a useful aid in identifying where improvements in the development process may be needed, especially if it identifies how time and resources were spent. Such a record can help justify the future acquisition of software development tools to improve the development process.

System Operation

System operation documentation describes how to operate the system. The primary audience is the staff involved in the day-to-day use of the system and may include persons in many different roles: end-user staff, computer operators, data-entry staff, and management users. Rarely, however, will a single manual be appropriate for the varied needs these roles represent. Reference manuals, tutorials, and other training materials fall into this category, but they will be dealt with in a separate section, to follow, on end-user training.

One difference between this documentation and system development documentation is that the former describes the operation of the final system resulting from the development process, while the latter documents the development process itself. Both have their utility, but their purposes are quite different. Each should be considered separately to avoid confusion to their readers or misdirected efforts in preparation.

The purpose of system operation documentation is to provide:

1. a current record of relevant information on the operation of the system from all staff perspectives involved;
2. a general overview of system capabilities, input requirements, and explanations of computer-generated outputs.

System Maintenance

System maintenance documentation differs from system operation documentation in that it is primarily oriented toward the future of the system and provides information useful to staff who may be involved in making subsequent revisions or corrections to the system.

Changes may be necessary to repair errors in the original system or because the requirements have been altered or extended. The audience for this documentation is primarily computer technical, that is, future developers. Parts of it may be end-users if the system includes capabilities for end-user customization and maintenance. These capabilities are discussed in Chapter 9.

The technical parts of this documentation may prove uninteresting reading, but the user should attempt to review it because its adequacy could affect the costs of future modifications and enhancements.

Software development methodologies such as *composite design* and *structured programming*, together with top-down approaches, inherently improve the maintainability of software systems. It is in your current and future interest to know what development standards and methodologies are being used by the developers. Discuss these topics with them and review the technical documentation to be sure these standards were applied.

INTEGRATED USER TRAINING

Providing adequate training for staff who will use the computer system is crucial to the successful operation of the system, but often it does not receive the attention it deserves. End-user management, being the most knowledgeable about external system requirements and the experience of staff who will use the system, should take primary responsibility for this function. Managers should see that adequate training is provided through manuals, classroom instruction, or actual experience using the system. Obviously, information will be required from the developers, who may even develop most of the training materials; however, this material should be carefully reviewed for appropriateness to the end-user staff, and management will need to arrange for its implementation. The developers are not always the best people to train end users, since they tend to emphasize the internal workings of the system rather than provide useful information on working through the system interfaces to get data in and out effectively.

There are several ways the computer can be used to assist in the training process. You may want to include some of these facilities in the requirements definition.

Computer-Produced Training Manuals

An obvious use of the computer is to employ its text editing capabilities to produce training and reference manuals. This task can be incorporated in the development process by making the development of the appropriate training or reference section a part of the required documentation for each function as it is designed and coded. With this approach, the user can review, edit, and revise the manual throughout the development process. A potential end user should be assigned to assist in the writing and review so that the desired level of communication is achieved. If this approach is used, I recommend that the user devise a table of contents for the manuals and include them as a part of the requirements definition. A project team approach with staff from both the end-user and software development areas can be effective for this task.

For large systems, consider separating the reference manual from the training manual. It is extremely difficult to produce a single document that will serve both purposes. Training manuals should be organized to take a person gently through the functions of the system using short exercises that are each complete in and of themselves. Training exercises should spare the user from discussions of intricate and rarely used features. Reference manuals, on the other hand, should be organized for quick and efficient access and should include discussions of every possible option available.

Text editing or word processing software can provide a flexible means of producing manuals. Sections can be readily added and, if necessary, revised, facilitating preparation of new sections as the system development progresses. The user thus benefits from early reviews of how the system will be used. Such a manual describes how to use the system in the language of the end user, or at least it should. This can provide a more meaningful picture of the system design than many of the technical descriptions the user is given to review. I was recently told by a user that he never really understood how the system would work until he saw the training manual, and that in the future he would specify that the training manual be the first document prepared.

Test Data Bases

Although adequate manuals assist in the training process, they rarely substitute for experience gained through actual system use. Many people, especially first-time computer users, approach the system with trepidation. They often fear that the consequences of a mistake will be a disaster such as destroying the entire data base. The creation of a small but realistic data base on which they can gain experience and confidence can overcome this problem. The test data base may contain a copy of a subset of *live* data, or it may contain *made-up* data. The primary condition is that it not be the real data base. The users should be told that it is not an original so they need not be concerned. They should also be told that the system is not supposed to break down as a result of a user error. Nevertheless, if a breakdown does occur, tell the developers so they can repair the system before the same thing happens in *live* operation.

The use of a smaller subset of the real data base has other advantages in a training environment. Response times will be faster and therefore outputs (including those generated by user errors) will be produced more rapidly. This fast response factor is important during the learning experience, since waiting a long time only to discover that a mistake was made can be distracting and frustrating. The computer cost incurred by processing large files and producing lengthy outputs is an unnecessary expense during training.

Test data bases can serve additional purposes:

1. system component and integration testing,
2. user acceptance testing,
3. testing of future revisions and modifications,
4. system demonstrations.

A test data base is especially important for training and demonstrations when data security and privacy considerations prevent the use of live data for these purposes.

Automated Help Functions

For on-line systems, a useful method for addressing the need for a reference manual is often to incorporate a *help* function within the interface system. The typical way a help function works is that at any point during an interaction with the computer system, an end user can press a *help* key and the software will display explanations of the current options available. The user's current activity is suspended while the help screens are viewed. The user can access related topics by indicating additional selections on each help screen. When the user finishes reading the help screens, the system returns to exactly the same point the user was at before pressing the *help* key.

Including an on-line help function is sometimes a good way to accommodate both experienced and casual end users without the need for two different interfaces. For example, when the computer detects an input error, a short error message might be displayed. Experienced users are likely to be familiar with these messages and understand immediately what should be done to correct the error. Casual users, who would not understand the cause of the error, could press the *help* key to display a fuller explanation of why the input was found to be in error and the steps that should be taken to correct it. This approach avoids annoying the experienced user with unnecessary explanations that impede her or his work.

Depending on the complexity of the system interface, a help function may increase the development costs, but often these costs are quickly recovered by more effective use of the system in operation and by reductions in the costs of preparing and maintaining up-to-date reference manuals.

Computer-Assisted Training

Software can be provided to lead a trainee through the learning process in a self-paced interactive mode. This software may be developed in conjunction with the application system, in which case a user is presented with exercises and intructions on what to do. Often the tutorial systems are separate from the associated application system and simulate the real system responses. In such instances, coordination is required between the two when changes are made to application system.

Generalized course writer software is also available. This allows you to develop your own training materials, such as explanatory text or test questions and answers, and to specify the training paths—that is, which sections should be represented when a question is answered incorrectly. The trainee is then presented with this material in an on-line mode. The use of this type of software should be supplemented with actual experience on the real system, and example exercises in the training package must also be kept up to date as revisions are made to the application system. This approach is rarely cost-effective unless a large number of new end users must be trained on the system on a regular basis. If the following considerations apply in your organization, computer-assisted training may be worthwhile.

Clearly, many end users will need to be trained before the costs of developing a computer-assisted training facility can be justified. Some additional considerations are listed below:

1. End-user training will be an ongoing activity.
2. End users have an aversion to studying manuals but may be enthusiastic about an interactive approach.
3. Organized rather than self-directed study is desirable, but the number of trainees at any one time is too low to justify the cost of formal instruction periods.
4. The costs of developing training software can be spread over a long period and over many users.

HUMAN-FRIENDLY INTERFACES

Earlier sections of this book discussed several possible approaches to developing an interface between the computer and the end users. In this section, the major characteristics of each approach are summarized, including ways to make each of them more friendly—that is, simpler to use.

Conversation Mode

In conversation mode, the computer system prompts the user with a series of questions, to which the user supplies an answer. This mode is most useful for portions of the system that will have infrequent users whose volume of input is small. The major disadvantage is the time required to display each question, which can be frustrating to the experienced user who is already aware of the next entry and views as a nuisance the time spent waiting for each question. One idea to improve this situation is to allow the user to specify a desired prompting level, such as terse or novice. In terse mode, prompts can be reduced to a few characters and several prompts can be combined. In novice mode, the system displays the full prompt and, possibly, explanations of the available options.

Figure 24 shows examples of prompts for a portion of a payroll system.

Novice mode:

> *Enter next employee number (6 digits):*
>
> *Enter employee name (up to 40 characters):*
>
> *Enter salary (include 2 decimal places):*

Terse mode:

> *Emp#?*
>
> *Name?*
>
> *Sal?*

Or even one prompt for all three entries:

> *Emp# / Name / Sal?*

Figure 24: Prompts for a payroll system

Menu mode

In menu mode, the computer displays a selection of available choices and the user selects one by entering the corresponding code or by pointing to or touching the appropriate spot on the screen. Again, experienced and frequent users of the system may become frustrated by successive display of familiar menus. There should be a way to enter all of the levels of choices, if they are known, without wading through many menu levels. The menu approach is useful for selecting various system functions and predefined output reports like those shown in Figure 25.

Select a function: ____

A. *Enter sales leads*
B. *Enter sales orders*
C. *Customer inquiry*
D. *Product inquiry*
E. *Sales Forecasts*

Different second-level menus may then be displayed after the first choice is made.

After choice C:

Which customer data? ____

1. *Name and address*
2. *Outstanding orders*
3. *Billing status*
4. *Sales history*

Enter customer number?

After choice D:

Which product data? ____

1. *Description and price*
2. *Inventory status*
3. *Sales summary by industry*
4. *Sales summary by region*

Enter product number?

Figure 25: Menus for a sales management system

Users who are familiar with the system could be allowed to enter all the information on the main menu, such as C4 followed by a customer number, thereby avoiding the display of the intermediate-level menus.

Command Mode

In command mode, the user enters a series of commands and parameters. This mode generally requires more familiarity with the system, since individual prompts and menus are not displayed. But it also permits more flexibility than the question and answer conversational approach and often leads to higher productivity for experienced system users. The types of commands will depend on the nature of the task, but they generally consist of keywords and parameters supplied by the user. The following list may provide some general guidelines for designing command languages. In the examples, keywords are shown in uppercase and the parameter data supplied by the user are shown in lowercase.

1. The commands should employ common words and, for the benefit of experienced users, should also permit these words to be abbreviated.

    Examples: LIST REPORT = Sales OUTPUT = terminal
    L R = sales O = t
    List R = product NUMBER = 20134 O = t

2. The entry of the commands should be in a free format. That is, parts of the command do not need to begin or end in specific positions on the command line and keywords do not have to appear in any particular order.

    Examples: LIST REPORT = sales OUTPUT = terminal
    LIST OUTPUT = terminal REPORT = sales

3. Multiple spaces between words should be permitted but should carry no special meaning. If possible, commas should be allowed, but not required, to accommodate individual styles.

    Examples: LIST   OUTPUT = printer, REPORT = a,b,c
    LIST OUTPUT = printer REPORT = a b c

4. Different but similar commands should have the same basic structure. When a parameter has the same meaning in different commands, the same keyword should be used.

Examples: SORT REPORT = sales ORDER = customer-name
OUTPUT = newreport
LIST REPORT = newreport OUTPUT = terminal

5. If the system is to supply default values for parameters omitted in the command, the values chosen should be sensible, predictable, and benign. For example, the default value for OUTPUT may be *terminal* as the most often desired destination for output. If REPORT is not specified, the default should not be to list the entire data base—a choice that can hardly be considered benign. When logical default values are not possible, it is better not to use them.

6. Where possible, commands and parameters should accept both uppercase and lowercase entries as equivalent. If synonyms for some commands are in common use, then they should all be allowed.

Examples: STOP, QUIT, END, LOGOFF, LOGOUT, BYE could all be used to end a terminal session.

Skeletal-Screen Mode

In skeletal-screen mode, the system displays row and column headings and the user fills in the blanks. This approach is useful for high-volume data entry when the same data items are being updated in many different records on the data base. An example of using skeletal-screen mode for handling annual salary increases affecting a large number of employees is shown in Figure 26.

Considerable attention should be given to the user interface part of the system. The mode of interface that functions best will depend on the nature of the tasks to be performed and the level of experience of the end users. As the computer industry has matured, software has become increasingly friendly to end users.

Employee Number	Employee Name	% Salary Change
0012345	Beauregard, G.	_____
0103068	Fitzgerald, F.	_____
. . .	. . .	. . .
1026558	Whitherspoon, R.	_____

Figure 26: Skeletal-screen data entry

The natural progress of the works of man is from rudeness to convenience, from convenience to elegance, and from elegance to nicety.

—Samuel Johnson,
The Idler

Software interfaces have, in recent years, moved from outright rudeness toward convenience. We can look forward to increasing levels of elegance and nicety in the future.

Chapter 9

PLANNING FOR CHANGE

The old order changeth, yielding place to the new.
—Alfred, Lord Tennyson,
The Passing of Arthur

CHANGES IN FUNCTIONAL REQUIREMENTS

The techniques and tools employed by the software developers can affect the future flexibility of the system. To ensure that suitable methods are used that will allow your software system to accommodate changes in your external system, you should include in the requirements definition information concerning which areas of the specifications are likely to change over time. The design proposal produced by the developers should address the issue of how these changes will be incorporated in the future.

Automated Maintenance Systems

Both the data and the processes may require modification during the life of the system. The design specification may include requirements for an automated end user-oriented maintenance capability. Such a facility will permit end users to modify some properties of the system directly without a need for programming intervention. To achieve this level of flexibility, the user should specify which parts of the system are subject to change and through what type of interface these

115

changes are to be made to the system. Some types of changes are likely to occur on short notice and therefore should be planned in advance. These changes should be accommodated by the system without a need for reprogramming.

Depending on the scope and complexity of the system, the maintenance component may require the establishment of needs, goals, and objectives with a future perspective of several years. The specifications should include which system parameter data values and processing rules are subject to change, and the requirements for incorporating them, such as response times, costs, and security considerations.

The security measures employed for entering modifications to system parameters are typically greater than those for routine system input, since an inappropriate change in the value of a system parameter can have far-reaching effects. Often, maintenance system use is restricted to a few key staff members, usually at the supervisory or management level.

Program Independence

Program independence means that programs are written to be free of specific data values; that is, when a data value is required by the program, it is obtained from a parameter file. The use of a parameter file permits data values to be modified without changing the actual program. In earlier years, hardware costs were much higher in relation to labor costs for software development, and data values tended to be embedded directly in the software programs. Such a situation is no longer defensible because computer hardware costs have decreased and storage access speeds have dramatically increased. Any time gained in machine efficiency by embedding such parameter values directly in the program modules will be lost (usually by many orders of magnitude) the first time a change in a parameter value is required, since a modification of the program will be required to change the data value. If these values are stored on files, like other application data, then updating them can also be an end-user function rather than a programmer function. Parameter files offer a means to an automated maintenance system if software is developed to allow the end user to update the values in the file.

The advantages of using parameter files are summarized below:

1. identifies and separates from the programs those details that are likely to change over time or installations;
2. provides a planned mechanism to accommodate future changes in specifications;
3. provides an end-user tool for incorporating changes, thereby minimizing future programming intervention;
4. makes planned and orderly change an integrated part of the system;
5. provides the user a wide variety of options over time, and allows the system to serve multiple users, each having a customizing capability;

Commercially available application development tools often incorporate the use of parameter files. If these packages are used in the development process, the resulting application may include this kind of flexibility.

On-line inquiry and report writer packages allow the end-user to define new file inquiries and design new report formats. The end user can also determine which subsets of the data base are to be included in the report, what sequence the report is in, which data items are displayed, and how the report is to be formatted. These packages vary in their ease of use, some still requiring programmer-level expertise.

Generalized data entry packages provide an ability to construct different screen formats for each type of transaction, a feature known as forms editing. Forms editor packages also permit various levels of data item editing specifications to be incorporated. Again, some of these packages may require programmer-level expertise, but they can greatly speed up the application development process.

Data base management systems often include components for on-line inquiry, report writing, and forms editing. These packages also provide security options, such as passwords for gaining access to each function and type of data item. The operating system itself, or a terminal management system that works with the operating system, provides password checking and file access security, although not generally any lower than file level.

Parameter files can be used to provide flexibility for a variety of different elements of the system. Examples of parameter files that the end user can modify as required are shown below.

Interface Specifications:

1. system prompts
2. system error messages
3. output labels for data items
4. report headings
5. report sequences
6. *help* text

Operational Specifications:

1. system processing schedules
2. output distribution
3. priority of tasks and users
4. hardware configuration (location of printers, types of terminals)

Machine Independence

Computer programming instructions are written in machine-sensible languages. Some languages are specific to certain computers, and systems developed in these languages can therefore only be used on compatible hardware. Other languages share industry-wide standards and can be implemented on a variety of computers. The choice of programming language is based on various technical considerations such as suitability for the type of application processing. However, the user should be aware of the language's portability (or lack thereof) among computer systems in the event that changes in the hardware environment become desirable. If portability is required, include that specific objective in the design specification. You should state for which manufacturer's hardware, which classes of machines, which terminals, and which personal computer interfaces you are interested in having such provisions made.

Application software is often built using the facilities of generalized system software packages, such as data base management systems, terminal management systems, and application generators. Some of these packages are specific to certain hardware, so the portability requirements must be applied to the use of these packages as well.

If the programming language used is not available on a variety of computers, your option to change computers in the future is restricted. The use of a portable language does not always guarantee portability, as machine dependencies have insidious ways of creeping into the program code. The most likely areas for this to occur are in file access methods that are provided by some, but not all, operating systems, or in taking advantage of special hardware devices that may not be available on other machines.

If the software requirements include portability among operating systems and machines, then modules that must include nonportable code should be carefully identified and isolated from the remainder of the system, in order that the least effort be required to move the system to other environments. Ask that the design proposal include estimates for redeveloping these specific program modules should the system need to be moved to different hardware or operating systems.

CHANGES IN DATA REQUIREMENTS

Data Independence

With program independence from specific data item values, provided in part through the use of parameter files, software gains a degree of flexibility. That is, parameter data values may be changed independently of changing the programs. However, the programs still have to know where the data values are stored and how to retrieve them. If a program expects to find a data value at a certain location in the data base, then any format changes to the data base will require a program modification.

Data dependence requires that when a change is made to the storage device or the format of the stored data, the program be changed. Data independence does not require a program change because the information on where the data is stored and how it is retrieved is not embedded in the program.

Data base management systems serve to isolate the program from the specifics of data storage and retrieval. The program simply requests the data items it requires and the data base management system supplies them. The flexibility gained by this data independence means that new data items can be added and that those programs that do not require these new data items will continue to function without modification. Commercially available data base management systems achieve varying degrees of data independence. Their flexibility may not be unlimited, but their options are much greater.

Data base management systems have other advantages, and their use typically results in considerably faster application development.

1. Data entry and data storage requirements are reduced because data can be stored once and shared by many different applications, as in payroll and accounting.
2. Problems of data inconsistency are avoided by reducing data redundancy.
3. Data integrity can be maintained by defining validation procedures to be applied each time a storage operation is attempted by an application program, rather than depending on each and every program to validate all conditions properly.
4. Many common functions are incorporated in data base management systems, eliminating the need to develop them within each application. Those functions include backup and restoration of files, security provisions, and inquiry and report writing capabilities.

Data Dictionaries

A data dictionary, itself a data base, contains the definitions of the data items stored in the application data bases. It serves as a repository for the types of information normally included in the design specification relating to data item formats. Data base software that supports a data dictionary usually allows the user to determine what additional information may be stored in the dictionary. The basic set of information applies to each data item: its size, which input transactions it is in, which outputs it is in, its internal name, its external label, which program modules reference it, and so forth. Keeping track of this type of information for large and complex systems requires an automated system; "data dictionary" is the term used to describe such a system.

A data dictionary is a data and system documentation tool that can be used to advantage during all phases of system development, including the requirements definition phase. The ten-step plan presented in Chapter 5 can be greatly facilitated by making use of data dictionary capabilities to store and analyze the information produced in each step.

The major advantages of a data dictionary are that it:

1. provides a tool for centrally managing *data about data*;
2. provides common language definitions of the function and use of data items;
3. answers questions about each data item:
   a. where is it stored?
   b. what is its source?
   c. where is it used?
   d. what are its valid values?
   e. who can modify it?
   f. who can access it?
   g. which reports contain it?
   h. which transactions contain it?
4. answers questions about the internal system structure:
   a. which programs reference which other programs?
   b. which programs use which data items?
   c. which programs produce which reports?
   d. which data items are contained in each report?
   e. which programs process which transactions?
   f. which data items are contained in each transaction?

Data dictionaries are often integrated with data base management systems. In this case, they are referred to as *active* dictionaries, meaning that changes to the programs or the data base are automatically reflected in the dictionary. For example, if *which programs use which data items* is part of the information contained in the dictionary, then when a program is modified to reference a new data item, this fact is automatically recorded in the dictionary by the software. With data dictionaries that are not an integral part of a data base management system (referred to as *stand-alone* or *passive* dictionaries), such facts have to be entered into the dictionary independently of changing the program. These dictionaries will not reflect the status of the system and its data unless they are conscientiously updated. *Active* and *user-expandable* data dictionaries are often available as an additional component of a data base management system.

Companies regard their employees and equipment as valuable resources and devote the necessary time and money to manage them effectively. As data becomes recognized as a valuable resource, dictionaries become more widely used as a means for central management of large, complex, and shared data bases. Active data dictionaries allow changes to be made in one place and the effects of those changes to be reflected throughout the system software.

APPLICATION INTEGRATION AND EVOLUTION

The earlier sections of this chapter discussed what techniques may be used to increase future flexibility in handling changes in data and processing requirements. Another type of change that may be anticipated is system evolution into entirely new levels of needs and goals. Planning for this type of change is made easier by understanding the typical evolution of systems in organizations.

Operational-level Support Systems

Typically, companies make those functions that are labor-intensive and repetitive in nature the first candidates for automation—payroll and accounting systems are two examples. These applications support the operational-level functions of the company. They are commonly well-defined, were previously done manually, and produce tangible final products like paychecks, bank statements, and invoices. The day-to-day users of these systems are the operational-level employees within the functional areas of the company.

As more applications are automated within a company, people begin to realize that many data items are common to several applications. If the systems are independent, this data is collected, encoded, and entered into each system redundantly. Not only is the effort inefficient, but if the input values differ more effort is required to reconcile and correct them. Similar problems occur with outputs. If one system derives data items that become input to another application, and if the transfer is accomplished by manual reentry, the possibility of introducing errors is increased. These problems are most easily eliminated if the various applications share a common data base.

The sharing of data, of course, introduces other complications, like data protection and security, that must be addressed. Agreements have to be reached within the external system, such as who is responsible for updating which data items. Data base management systems provide facilities to handle many of these problems.

Management Information Systems

Once a sufficient number of inter-related applications is automated, the possibility exists of generating new levels of information that are applicable to higher-level managerial functions. If the information from this "critical mass" of applications can be combined, then new types of integrated summary information may be produced that were never practical within the context of manual systems. Managers are the day-to-day users of this level of systems.

Historically, managers have been less exposed to computers than have operational-level staff; therefore, they frequently fail to take advantage of the type of information that computers make available. As personal computers make their way into managers' offices, managers will demand more of this type of information. But by that time, it may be too late to ensure that this data is readily available, since each application may have been automated independently, without consideration of future management-level needs, and software integration may be extremely difficult and may only be possible by starting over. Management should be aware of the constraints that may be placed on its ability to obtain management-level information at some future time if automation occurs without a central planning component within the organization. The current trend toward stand-alone mini- and microcomputer systems to handle single applications will further increase the obstacles to developing comprehensive management information systems. The central planning function should help users obtain the computing resources they require, but from an organizationwide perspective.

Distributed processing offers another alternative to moving computing power toward end-user control without creating incompatible system environments. In a *distributed* system, data bases are stored on a central mainframe computer, from which they can be shared by many users. The required subsets of the data base can be distributed to smaller satellite computers, including personal computer work stations, where local functions can be performed. With the advent of local area networks, programs and data can be freely exchanged among all systems connected to the network.

Business Planning Systems

Once an organization has management information systems in place, historical data from many aspects of the business can be compared and correlated. The higher-level executives may then want to use this data for future planning. They will be interested in finding out which areas of the operation need improvement, which areas may be threatened by future economic conditions, how profits may be affected by certain economic trends, and so on.

The wealth of historical data on business operations provided by management information systems can be integrated with externally available information, such as stock market figures, census data, and economic indicators, to assist with business planning functions. This data can be accessed by a variety of modeling systems to produce spreadsheet analysis, graphics, and other types of reports.

Some analyses may require historical data across many years, and until the management information systems have been in place long enough, the available data on which to base long-term trend analysis may be inadequate. Nonetheless, their potential benefits make business planning systems a natural extension of management information systems.

Traditionally, software development within an organization has occurred application by application. The problems associated with integrating information from multiple applications have been addressed only after substantial investments in software have been made. Management information systems can rarely be based on data from a single application developed originally to provide operational-level support. The task of combining data from many sources, each differently organized and structured from the viewpoint of a single application, becomes increasingly formidable and often requires substantial new investment in redesign and reprogramming of existing systems before management information systems can be attempted.

To the extent that the proliferation of application-specific data bases can be avoided in the first place, future integration will be easier and management information systems will be far less expensive to implement. The number of applications a company might automate is great, perhaps becoming boundless in the foreseeable future. If the data bases are organized along application lines, then the number of data bases continues to expand, ultimately leading to integration costs that are difficult to justify. Conversely, the number of *subjects* of interest to a company is much smaller than the number of potential applications, and data bases organized around these subjects will grow slowly and reach a plateau. Typical subjects in a company are personnel, products, accounts, customers, orders, vendors, and so on. Each application may use data from several subject data bases, as shown in Figure 27. Once the subject data bases are developed, new

Applications: (Subject Data Bases:)	ACCOUNTS	PRODUCTS	PARTS	VENDOR	CUSTOMERS	ORDERS	PERSONNEL
Purchasing	X		X	X			
Inventory Control		X	X			X	
Sales		X			X	X	
Order Entry		X			X	X	
Shipping		X			X	X	
General Ledger Accounting	X						X
Payroll	X						X
Billing		X			X	X	
Accounts Receivable	X				X	X	
Accounts Payable	X		X	X			
Production Scheduling		X	X			X	X

Figure 27: Applications and subject data bases used

applications can be added by using or augmenting existing data bases, rather than through continual data base proliferation. The number of applications will grow far more rapidly than the number of subjects.

The data stored in these subject data bases can be summarized and viewed in new ways to satisfy management information and business planning system requirements. The operational-level applications can remain in place and unchanged while new systems are developed that quickly extract the relevant data for these data bases. Often management information and long-range planning needs only require high-level summaries of large amounts of data and not, in fact, the precision of up-to-the-minute data values; therefore, the extractions may take place at various time intervals—daily or weekly for example—depending on the needs.

You should plan for an incremental and orderly build-up of application systems and subject data bases. Once a *customer* data base is established containing basic customer data such as name, address, and type of business, a simple customer information system can be developed to allow end users to ask questions like: how many customers are located in the southeast; how many hospitals buy our products; and which state contains the greatest number of customers. Later, when the product and order data bases are developed, a sales information system can be developed using all three data bases to answer questions such as: which type of business places the largest dollar volume of sales; which products sell best in the winter months; and who were the top ten customers last month.

Do not try to develop all-embracing information systems all at once. Build them individually, as the applications that create the necessary data on the subject data bases are in place and functioning well. Approaching the development of a corporate data base along subject lines keeps the number of data bases from getting out of control. Furthermore, the integration will be occurring as each new application that uses or augments the data on these data bases is developed. The integration will not have been deferred to the end when it may be too costly to achieve. The development resources can be expended on new applications and extensions to management information and business planning systems, rather than on redesigning and redeveloping existing systems.

The use of appropriate tools and methodologies in the software development process is critical to achieving these results. An organization also needs an overall information processing strategy to make sound investments in present systems and to control future costs. The acquisition of personal computers and minicomputers dedicated to single applications should be planned carefully so that the future integration required for higher-level application systems is not prohibited. The hardware selected should have communications compatibility across end-user and application lines.

As a user developing design specifications for an operational-level application, you may want to make certain that your system can evolve in the future along with the growth of the company and its overall use of computers.

Figure 28 summarizes the typical evolution of computer applications within organizations. It shows who the end users are and the

Application	Type of user	Tools and methods
Operational-level support systems	Operational staff and supervisors	Machine independence through industry-standard languages
		Program independence through use of parameter files
		Data independence through data base management systems
Management information systems	Managers and executive staff analysts	Data base management systems through shared data bases
Business planning systems	Executives and their staff analysts	Data dictionaries through centralized and standardized data definitions

Figure 28: Application levels, users, and methods

types of tools and methodologies that help achieve the goals of each application and build a solid foundation for the next level.

The failure of most management information system efforts can be traced to overly ambitious objectives and the lack of a solid application foundation on which to build. If you are the user charged with developing management information system requirements, attempt to identify concrete information needs, make certain that appropriate software development tools and methods are used, and build the system incrementally. Do not try to achieve everything in one step. As Confucius said:

The firm, the enduring, the simple, and the modest are near to virtue.

Part Four

HOW TO INCREASE MANAGEMENT PRODUCTIVITY THROUGH COMPUTERS

"Just pass the work I assign you along to somebody else and trust to luck. We call that delegation of responsibility. Somewhere down near the lowest level of this coordinated organization I run are people who do get the work done when it reaches them, and everything manages to run smoothly without too much effort on my part. I suppose that's because I am a good executive. Nothing we do in this large department of ours is really very important, and there's never any rush. On the other hand, it is important that we let people know we do a great deal of it."

—Joseph Heller,
Catch 22

Chapter 10

TARGET AREAS FOR END-USER COMPUTING

TRENDS IN TECHNOLOGY

Direct use of the computer as a tool by people who are not members of information systems (IS) or data processing departments has spread in recent years. The increased computer use by non-IS professionals has been fostered by advances in both hardware and software technologies.

From the hardware side, the availability of low cost and increasingly powerful personal computers and work stations has afforded organizations the ability to provide computing resources on a much broader scale without consuming equivalent scarce mainframe resources. Favorable price-performance ratios for current minicomputers have also helped pave the way for departmental computing systems. Many of these systems require little of the daily computer-operations functions that are typical of mainframe computers. These systems can often be serviced by operations specialists on a part-time basis. Their primary requirements are operating system installation and tuning; application software installation; backing up of user files and data bases; and installation, maintenance, and upgrade of peripheral devices as required. They generally function in normal office environments without the need for special physical facilities.

From the software side, the availability of a new generation of software tools has coincided with the introduction of new hardware. These tools are aimed at tasks performed by a broader base of personnel than information systems professionals. Three areas where the new software has become important are office automation, decision support, and executive information systems.

IMPROVING COMMUNICATIONS THROUGH OFFICE AUTOMATION SYSTEMS

Office Automation (OA) or Office Support (OS) systems typically include facilities for electronic mail, document preparation, calendaring or time management, automated address and telephone lists, and maintenance of tickler files. Parts of these systems may be used by all levels within an organization: secretarial, administrative, specialists, and management. The most successful component of these systems to date has been electronic mail, followed by document preparation, particularly for clerical and technical personnel.

A recent report from the Office of Technology Assessment, "Technology and the American Economic Transition: Choices for the Future," found that while only 17 percent of companies with annual sales less than $1 million use electronic mail, nearly 60 percent of those with annual sales over $1 billion do so. The survey also presented the following results describing the pattern of usage:

Percentage of Electronic Mail:	Replaces:
55%	telephone calls
10%	telex
5%	first-class mail, courier, and other electronic means.

They also found that 20 percent of the electronic mail falls into a new category generated by other computer technology such as mailing electronic spreadsheets built by decision support systems.

IMPROVING PLANNING THROUGH DECISION SUPPORT SYSTEMS

Decision Support Systems (DSS) consist primarily of spreadsheets, graphics packages, project management systems, and financial modeling software. They are aimed at staff specialists involved in business planning, model building, and "what if" analysis. The packages in

DSS generally contain tool-oriented software with analytical capabilities that are applicable to a large set of highly specialized tasks. They are often aimed at individual productivity gains.

Many tasks that previously required professional programmers can now be automated by the end user directly through these tools. Many information systems departments have responded to this new group of customers by setting up information centers where users can go for training and assistance in using and applying the software. These information centers may also provide training and support for the office automation systems.

Information centers have been around long enough that their evolutionary patterns can be seen. They usually begin with a small staff—often as few as one—whose responsibilities include setting up a library and a "hot-line," publishing a newsletter, and offering training on personal computer products and a few mainframe products such as electronic mail. As computer literacy spreads through the organization, the information center expands into other areas such as providing services for micro-mainframe links, mainframe-based fourth-generation languages, data extracts and downloads, and centralized coordination of software purchases. As the users become more sophisticated, they want still more services, such as those relating to departmental minicomputers: assistance with hardware and system software installation, performance tuning, and backup procedures. Information centers will continue to expand as end users get more comfortable with computers and computers become easier to use. In a few organizations, they have expanded to the point where they have outlived their usefulness and been dismantled. Users have often become so dependent on the information centers that high-level analysts perform routine operations and maintenance tasks. At this point, some organizations have decided to return these responsibilities to the departments that need them and have them manage their own technology.

Decision support software is generally not used by senior management within an organization, who tend to have little time to learn the intricacies and subtleties required to make it perform useful work. This software has powerful functionality, but that comes with the price of complexity of operation. Senior management frequently delegates the operation of systems using this software to staff personnel.

IMPROVING TRACKING AND CONTROL THROUGH EXECUTIVE INFORMATION SYSTEMS

An even newer class of software has been gaining use within large corporations: Executive Information Systems (EIS), also called executive support systems (ESS). As with any emerging field, this one has been defined in many different ways. Some corporations define it as electronic mail, office automation, spreadsheets, decision support, or combinations of all of the above. While EIS may share a few components with these systems, or more appropriately, may be integrated with some of their components, executive information systems are focused on quite different objectives.

Figure 29 illustrates some of the differences between executive information systems and decision support systems.

In their recent book, "Executive Support Systems," John F. Rockart and David W. DeLong, of the Center for Information Systems Research (CISR) at MIT's Sloan School of Management, present five key factors influencing the need for executive information systems:

1. the globalization of companies, creating a need to manage subsidiaries as a single organization that requires more information than was previously available;
2. personnel cost cutting, specifically at the middle management levels that previously produced many of the status reports;
3. worldwide use of communications, particularly electronic mail, which brings more diverse information to headquarters;
4. advances in computer technology;
5. the rate of change in technology.

Executive information systems often share some attributes of office automation, particularly the need for communications capabilities among users. An EIS should therefore be able to interface with an electronic mail system. Preferably, users will have the capability to send screens containing graphs and other data that point out something of importance, such as a problem area, and to annotate these screens with questions, interpretations, or other observations to accompany the mail.

An EIS must also manage textual data. Data displays must often be linked to management narratives that explain or amplify the data.

	Decision Support	Executive Information
End User	Staff specialists, e.g., financial planners, analysts	Senior executives and managers and their staffs
Usage Pattern	Frequent and repetitive (several hours per day)	Infrequent and sporadic (several times per week)
Data Emphasis	Quantitative data used for tactical decision making; primarily internal financial and schedule data.	Time-series and qualitative data used for strategic decision making; numeric and narrative data from both internal and external sources
End User Task Focus	Planning, modeling, "what if" tasks; individual productivity	Monitoring performance, forecast; identifying problem areas; individual and group productivity
Function-ality	Data-intensive, model-oriented; powerful analytical capability; large volume of numerical data; support for single users	Data retrieval-oriented, information compression, trend analysis; links to narrative data; support for group communications
End User Training	Frequent usage and powerful analytical capability justifies training investment	Intuitive interface minimizes training requirements

Figure 29: Differences between decision support systems and EIS

Such communications are critical for synthesizing the responses and commentary of other managers and analysts to "fill out the picture" presented to the executives. For example, a CEO may want to have access to the narrative provided by the CFO while viewing this month's cash flow statement.

Unlike the majority of decision support systems, executive information systems must be able to combine data effectively from a variety of sources. Financial data such as monthly actuals versus budgets will undoubtedly be required to effectively monitor the company's performance and current status. However, this data should be augmented with that from external sources—such as competitor news and financials, regulatory news, economic indicators, political changes, and other external factors—that may affect the company's business objectives.

Executive time is at a premium. Systems that provide yet more data to the already overburdened executive will not be welcomed. An effective EIS must therefore provide new and better information yet less volume of data per se. In fact, *the goal of EIS is to provide information rather than data.* The executive requires a system that compresses information through filtering mechanisms such as exception-reporting, which calls attention to areas that are performing better or worse than expected (i.e., outside some user-defined tolerance interval). It may be important to know what is going exceptionally well as well as what is going badly. The executive can then focus attention quickly on problem areas, view them in contrast to the success areas, and review those subsets of data more intensively.

Another requirement of EIS is minimal end-user training. Executives may use the system sporadically, or they may use it frequently for brief review periods. The user interface should be friendly and intuitive to reduce both initial training and the need for relearning. The interface should also minimize, if not completely eliminate, keyboard usage. Many executives have limited keyboard skills. In addition, the use of a command-level syntax requires more training than is appropriate for executive computer use. The most successful systems to date make extensive use of menus accessible with a mouse, touch-screen, or other pointing devices.

As discussed more fully in a later chapter, the development side of the system should also provide a large degree of flexibility that will easily support rapid prototyping and modification as requirements change over time. Executives need to focus their attention on both short- and long-term company objectives; and their information needs can change quickly. The software behind the system must also be flexible—easy to build and to modify.

Chapter 11

FACTORS PROMOTING SUCCESSFUL EXECUTIVE INFORMATION SYSTEMS

SUPPORT REQUIREMENTS

Senior management support, i.e., an executive champion, remains the single most important key to success. Rockart and DeLong found that organizations that have implemented a successful EIS without a committed executive champion have been rare. Based on their case studies of thirty companies that have been involved in designing an EIS for their executives, Rockart and DeLong deemed the following factors important to successful implementation of an EIS:

1. a committed and informed executive sponsor
2. an operating sponsor
3. appropriate information systems staff
4. appropriate technology
5. management of data
6. clear link to business objectives
7. management of organization resistance
8. management of system evolution and spread

If these factors are categorized according to whether they have a high or a low management influence and a high or a low technology influence, as in Figure 30, they split evenly into the high and low technology categories; however, seven of the eight have a high-level management component.

Implementing an EIS successfully requires a high level of management skills, support, and involvement. Success will depend as much on management capability as on technological capability, if not

Influence	High Management	Low Management
High Technology	IS Staff Accessibility to data System Expansion	Hardware and Software Choices
Low Technology	Executive Champion Operating Sponsor Managing Resistance Links to Business Objectives	

Figure 30: Management and technology influences on success factors

more. These factors are discussed in more detail in the sections that follow.

An "Executive Champion"

Few EIS projects have succeeded without the leadership of a strong, committed executive. Ideally, this "executive champion" should be the most senior of target end users. He or she should devote as much time as possible to managing and monitoring the EIS implementation, including authorizing the necessary hardware and software resources and the personnel needed to develop and maintain the system. During design and implementation, the champion will need to provide direction and feedback to the developers and target end users. One of the most critical of the champion's roles is to motivate the staff who will supply the necessary data feeds to the EIS. The data will come from a variety of sources within the organization, such as spreadsheets, hard-copy reports, and corporate as well as external data bases.

Staff who have previously viewed themselves as the "owners" of such data may be reluctant and uncooperative in this matter. Nearly everyone has come to believe that "information is power," and thus they may view the release of information as an erosion of a personal power base. The idea of automated feeding of this information to the highest levels of the organization, outside the "owner's" censorship and control, may be regarded with abject horror. So it may be imperative that the executive champion strongly communicate both company and personal interest in the success of the EIS to motivate those who supply the data to cooperate with the EIS development staff.

An "Operating Sponsor"

Because of the time required to manage the EIS development, and because of the busy schedule of a top executive, the executive champion often delegates day-to-day management of EIS development to a subordinate, known as the "operating sponsor." This person should be someone who can communicate with both the executive and the technical staff and translate business and technical information back and forth easily. He or she should also have easy access to the executive champion and the other target end users. The operating sponsor must have sufficient organizational clout and active support from the executive to ensure that impediments will not strangle the project. Thus one of the executive's senior managers or a senior staff person is a logical choice. The important criteria are that the sponsor be an enthusiast for the system and in a position to know the executive needs. Some organizations have been successful by developing the initial EIS applications for the staff management who support the senior executives rather than for the executives themselves.

Technical Staffing

The EIS project must have adequate resource levels. The number of people required will depend on both the initial scope of the project and whether an EIS package will be procured or the EIS developed in-house using existing lower-level tools.

The IS staff selected for the project should have an understanding of the business, as well as the technology, and be supportive rather than resistant to EIS. The most successful EIS implementations did not follow the typical system development life cycle. They depended far more on rapid prototyping, timely review and end-user feedback, and prompt redesign and re-presentation. Some IS staff may try to enforce traditional systems development methodology when it is in-appropriate for the project. Many successful executive information systems have been developed with little or no formal implementation plan, no traditional cost-justification phase, and no complete needs analysis. Some IS staff are not accustomed to this type of development and consequently may fear they are designing a poor-quality system. Prototyping as a design and development methodology is described more fully in a later chapter.

TECHNOLOGY ISSUES

Should an EIS be mainframe- or micro-based, or operate within a cooperative processing environment?

The major considerations affecting the hardware decision are:

1. hardware compatibility
2. system capacity
3. hardware costs
4. response time

Hardware Compatibility

   a. between the executive's home and office configuration,
   b. between end users who need to communicate with each other,
   c. between EIS hardware and corporate data base hardware to facilitate transfer of data.

If user-to-user communications are a requirement, an EIS must provide some type of link between end users, thereby eliminating a purely stand-alone microcomputer-based system. Each personal computer must be linked to others via a central computer or a network such as a Local Area Network (LAN).

Links with a mainframe computer also permit the executive to communicate with other, nonexecutive, staff, who are not connected to a LAN, through mainframe-based electronic mail systems.

Decision support or "DSS" tools are often purchased and used as individual productivity tools, whereas EIS applications are more likely to be used by a network of executives and senior managers to monitor and control the performance of the company and to communicate their ideas and concerns. Stand-alone personal computer software is less appealing when the system must support multiple end users with a consistent view of current status.

System Capacity Considerations:

    a. the number of end-users,
    b. the number and size of the executive data bases,
    c. the number of different menus, reports, charts, etc.

Systems that are primarily PC-based and use a LAN purely for user-to-user communications will usually have system capacity limitations. Since all the data that the executive may want to see will have to reside on each personal computer, the maintenance time required to keep the EIS data bases up to date will increase linearly with the number of executives who use the system. A more satisfactory approach is to have executives share EIS data bases from a common node of the network, a minicomputer, or the mainframe itself. This not only eliminates the problem of maintaining many different copies of the EIS data bases, but also ensures that all executives are viewing the same data. Data integrity is critical if the executives are to have confidence in the system.

Hardware Costs

The cost of hardware for executive workstations can be substantially lower when executives make use of common disk storage rather than require megabytes of disk storage at each workstation. Conversely, there are additional costs associated with transferring data to and storing it at each executive's machine. The time needed for data transfer can quickly become prohibitive as the EIS expands to more applications requiring additional data, and to more executives and managers within the organization.

Response Time

    a. interactive response time,
    b. maintenance time to update the EIS data bases and refresh the screens if necessary.

While response time may be adversely affected by other activities that take place simultaneously on a mainframe, there can be compensating factors. For example, retrievals from a high-speed mainframe disk drive are often considerably faster than those from personal computer disk drives, and the mainframe internal speed may also be faster than a personal computer for producing data aggregates for higher-level summaries.

Acceptable response time for information requests is critical to the success of EIS. Yet, the tendency is to underestimate the hardware and communications capacity requirements. Even though the response time may be adequate for an initial group of end users, it can rapidly deteriorate as the system expands to more users and larger data bases. Communications technology that is appropriate for high-volume transactional systems may not be adequate for interactive EIS applications.

Cooperative processing systems have some software components that operate on personal workstations and some that operate centrally on one node of a network, a minicomputer, or a mainframe. Such systems include a communications component to transfer data efficiently between the workstation and the central node or mainframe. If the software components are appropriately distributed between the two locations, the system can perform better than one that is entirely localized or centralized. The central node, mini-computer, or mainframe can be equipped with faster disk drives, faster processing units, and more memory than is feasible on each individual workstation.

What Software Capabilities Are Needed to Build an EIS?

The major software capabilities required are:

1. fast prototype development and enhancement ability,
2. centrally controlled maintenance capability,
3. an easy-to-use end-user interface,
4. acceptable response times.

The software used to build an EIS must provide a method for creating fast, flexible prototypes that can be modified quickly with minimal development effort.

The developers must also design a centralized maintenance capability that allows the system to expand readily to accommodate additional end users. Systems that are purely PC-based require that maintenance time expand linearly with the number of users and the size of their application data bases.

The software must also facilitate building of easy-to-use and intuitive interfaces for executive end users. Training requirements must be minimized.

Finally, executives require acceptable interactive response time during their normal sessions. The maintenance time required for updating their data bases must be reasonable and centrally managed.

Should an EIS have its own data base or should it have direct access to the corporate operational data bases?

Operational systems were developed to support operations such as order entry, billing, accounting, distribution, and payroll.

Information systems, on the other hand, require the ability to summarize, format, present, and analyze data. Such systems are normally provided through a set of end-user computing facilities to handle both standard and ad hoc queries, report formatting, and data analyses. These functions are often performed against a subset of corporate data that is extracted, copied, and summarized from operational systems data bases.

There are legitimate reasons to separate these data bases, and perhaps even the hardware on which they reside:

1. The performance of the operational systems is not disrupted by *executive's* ad hoc queries and analyses, which are unpredictable.
2. The information needed by the executives is not being changed as it is being used. The users have a need for an accurate, defined point-in-time slice of the data.
3. Operational data bases are optimized for high-volume updating such as transaction processing, and are not necessarily suitable for *ad hoc* queries by executive end users.

Current data base technology uses an indexing method on each field that is used as a search field on retrieval. Querying a data base using fields for which an index has been built is clearly faster than searching through all the records in a data base to find the ones that satisfy the query. However, record updating is slowed by the need to update numerous indices each time a record is added, deleted, or modified. Consequently, a given data base design can be optimized for either retrieval or update, but one is usually done at the expense of the other. For these reasons, operational-level systems, which have a high volume of updates, are typically optimized for efficient updating, maintaining indices on a minimal number of fields required for routine reporting. Information systems, on the other hand, require indices on numerous fields due to the ad hoc and unpredictable queries that may be made. EIS data base designs must be particularly sensitive to response-time requirements and therefore must be optimized for fast retrieval. The same data base product may be used for both types of applications, but the number of indexed fields in an EIS data base would be greater.

If frequent updating of the EIS data bases is required, they are often updated with only the most recent data from the operational data bases. When the update requirements are less frequent, the EIS data bases can be recreated in their entirety from the operational data bases. If adjustments must be made to prior data in the operational data base, the EIS data bases may also be recreated rather than updated.

DATA FEEDER SYSTEMS

Identifying the sources for data required by an EIS can be the most difficult of the implementation problems. Much of the needed qualitative data may not necessarity exist in automated form. Even when it does exist, it may reside within an individual's personal computer data base or spreadsheet. Getting access to data from these sources on a timely basis can be a challenge.

Data for an EIS comes from a variety of sources. So the data feeder systems must be timely, accurate, and complete. The process of implementing an EIS can often uncover serious problems in an organization's data infrastructure. Organizational units may encode data differently, use varied definitions for the same data, and apply inconsistent rules to aggregate data at higher summary levels. They may produce their data on incompatible schedules and with different periodicity. Any one of these problems can invalidate or seriously impede the accumulation of summary-level data required for an EIS.

Problems of this nature will have to be resolved before an EIS can be used to maximum advantage.

Consistent data collection intervals will need to be established so that the executive data bases can be refreshed from multiple sources in order to represent the picture of the organization at one point in time. The ongoing need of a data administrator for an EIS is evident.

The problems of data ownership and controlling access to sensitive data must also be addressed. Issues of data security are often in conflict with executive requirements for ease of system use. Security requirements may call for elaborate log-on and password schemes, but the executive may want to do little more than turn on a power switch. Script files that reside on the personal computer may be created to handle logging into the system automatically, but the Management Information Systems (MIS) department may take a dim view of this approach.

THE POLITICS OF EIS

An EIS is highly integral to the management process itself. It presents new opportunities to make substantial improvements in the way a company is managed. The development process itself can uncover institutional road blocks in the form of processes and people. Such changes and discoveries have the potential of creating both heroes and failures, and may present some quite unwelcome changes in the management style and processes of an organization.

The barriers that will be encountered during the EIS implementation are often more political than technical. As mentioned earlier, the "owners" of data can be territorial about it, viewing its release as an erosion of their personal power base within an organization. This territorial attitude will often be masked with concerns about data security. There are certainly legitimate issues relating to data security, but you need to be careful to distinguish the issues that are real from those that are self-serving.

If the EIS project is being carried out without the direct involvement and active support of the MIS department, there may be other obstacles erected from that quarter. The MIS department may raise concerns about machine utilization on the mainframe or proliferation of personal computers beyond their direct control, or they may insist that the system integrate with their standard communications and operating system architecture. The latter point can be a particularly difficult one, because often the existing architecture may not be suitable for the interactive level of response time required for executive end users.

Resistance can also come from subordinate managers who fear that executives will have access to too much information concerning their operations. They may fear that the information will be misused or misunderstood by higher-level executives who are further removed from day-to-day operations. Management of this resistance will involve combinations of approaches, both educational and political. Leadership, commitment, and enthusiasm from an executive champion will certainly help overcome some of this resistance. The EIS project team should strive to involve all the parties in some meaningful way in order to build ownership in the project in those areas likely to be resistant. Some companies have discovered that the inclusion of names and telephone numbers of the data suppliers on the screens has helped to overcome this resistance. People feel that they, as the suppliers of the data, still have some visibility with the executives.

The next chapter surveys EIS functionality that cuts across applications, information compression techniques, prototyping as a design and development methodology, approaches to defining the data requirements for EIS, and selecting application areas.

Chapter 12

DESIGN OF EXECUTIVE INFORMATION SYSTEMS APPLICATIONS

FUNCTIONAL REQUIREMENTS

"Minimal Training"

There are important differences between an executive's work and that of an operational-level manager. An operational-level system is likely to be integral to the routine functions of a department or functional area, e.g., accounting, personnel, or order-entry; consequently, operational end users will make use of the system on a regular and frequent basis. Once they are trained in the use of the system, they will use it often enough to remain high on their learning curve. Executives, on the other hand, spend much of their time in meetings, interacting with people, and traveling. They will use their systems sporadically; periods of disuse will be interrupted by brief but intense periods of activity. This very different usage pattern requires that the user interface meet new standards of intuitiveness. Training and familiarity requirements must be minimal or eliminated. The obvious requirements are that the EIS applications be menu-driven, using a mouse, touch-screen, or other pointing device, to eliminate any need for an end-user command language.

"Navigation Paths"

The executive will need to navigate quickly, easily, and coherently through many different levels of data, focusing on those areas where internal and external conditions require attention at the moment. This data-driven navigational capability must not only be intuitive to employ, it must also provide quick access to the data of immediate interest regardless of its level in the structure. An on-line "slide show" of hundreds of reports and graphs with no logical method of navigation and random access is not efficient for executives. An important feature of "navigation" is that the end users can easily discern where they are in the structure and how to get to what they want to see next— upward, downward, or laterally.

Another difference in the needs of executives as opposed to operational-level management, is the requirement for information compression and filtering. While the operational manager is responsible for a given set of functions and will want to look at the relevant data in depth and routinely, the executive does not have the time to study, analyze, and digest all the data that may affect the organization. We have already considered the unboundedness of such data and the constantly changing data requirements. The system must provide the executive with the appropriate levels of summary data and the intuitive methods to navigate quickly to more detailed levels in areas of current interest. This ability to provide a logical, high-speed review path through hierarchically oriented data structures has become known as "drill-down" capability.

The system should also automatically monitor status at the lower levels of detail and direct the executive's attention to those problem areas whether or not these items happen to be accessed via drill-down. Rather than starting with high-level summary data and drilling down for more details, the system monitors the status of all levels of the data and reports the exceptions. This functionality, known as "exception-reporting," is the converse of drill-down.

A common mistake is to refer to the simple process of color-coding variances as exception-reporting. But the two are not the same: exception reporting is much more comprehensive. For example, in a financial system using color-coding, the screens display year-to-date actual, budget, variance, and percent variance for all expense line items. The line item names are colored red if the year-to-date actual is over budget by more than 10 percent, and green if the year-to-date actual is under 10 percent of the budget. Line item names remain white if the actual numbers fall within the current trigger settings of plus or minus 10% of budget. They are colored red if actual exceeds budget by more than 10%, and green if actual falls short of budget by more than 10%. Offsetting variances at lower levels of detail can mask problems when the executive is viewing the top screen, thereby not drawing attention to some of the line items so that they will be reviewed via drill-down to lower levels.

True exception-reporting will provide additional reports of all items, regardless of level, that fall outside the triggers set by the end user. Triggers can be stated in percentages or absolute terms, such as 10 percent or $10,000. The end user may wish to be notified of exceptions when either the percentage or absolute variance is exceeded, or only when both conditions are true. Each end user may want to set different values for the triggers and may also want to modify them within a review session. The exception screen would guide the executive directly to those reporting levels that may require further investigation. Exception-reporting is an example of information compression and filtering. The monitoring of all items is performed by the system, saving the executive time and lessening the possibility of oversight. The goal of information compression is to find the "hot spots" by viewing the smallest amount of data.

Since the executive is generally responsible more for strategic-level planning than operational management, she or he will often want to view current data in the context of historical trends and forecasts. Graphic presentation of such data is often the most effective method for discerning and understanding trends and patterns over time.

Figure 31 summarizes the EIS functional requirements.

Information Compression

Navigation paths can be used to provide information compression. To illustrate how, let us take a budget monitoring system as an example of an EIS application that meets many of the requirements listed in Figure 31. This particular system monitors actual revenues and expenses against budget. The budgets have been prepared at the department level and then consolidated to the division and then company level. As shown in Figure 32, the top screen in the EIS application displays the company-level aggregated values for each line item category in the accounting system. Each row on the screen contains a line item description followed by the year-to-date budget for that line item, then the year-to-date actual for that line item, the absolute variance (actual–budget), and finally the percent variance.

Assume the exception triggers have been set at either + or −

Data Access	Interfaces	Information Compression	Display Modes
Internal and external data	Intuitive and easy to use	Efficient navigation via drill-down	Graphic presentation for trend analysis
Historical and forecast data	Links to electronic mail for communications	Highlight problems via exception-reporting	Combinations of qualitative and quantitative data for context

Figure 31: EIS functional requirements

Standard Diversified, Ltd.

	Budget YTD	Actual YTD	Variance	% Variance
Personnel Expenditures				
Salary				
Overtime				
Medical Insurance				
Life Insurance				
Recruiting Fees	745,000	830,000	95,000	12.75
. . .				

Figure 32: Sample top menu

10 percent or + or − $50,000. Any line items whose variances fall outside these triggers will be colored red or green as appropriate. At this point the executive can select a red line item, such as "Recruiting Fees," and view the next lower level of available detail. The new screen would then show the division-level aggregates for the "Recruiting Fees' account, shown in Figure 33.

When the triggers are applied to this data, the "Commercial Division" line item might be colored red, and the column entries on the same row will show the variances at the division level for the "Recruiting Fees" account. If the executive now points at "Commercial Division," yet another screen appears, Figure 34, showing the detail of this account at the department level.

The triggers will now be applied at this level of data and the executive will see that "Research and Development" is shown in red and that its overspending in this account created the variance shown on the top screen.

By viewing only a small number of screens, the executive has now determined that the "Research and Development" department within the "Commercial Division" has exceeded its "Recruiting Fees" budget by either 10 percent or $50,000 or both. If the executive now points at one of the values in the row, as opposed to the line item name, a graph showing the monthly variances of actual versus budget will be displayed. The trend chart may indicate that there was an unusual overrun earlier in the year but that costs have been running well under budget since that time. The executive may now be satisfied that this matter does not deserve further attention and return to the top screen to pursue other paths.

Drill down capability can be used to spot and further investigate areas that are performing better or worse than expected. While this capability is useful and illustrates a form of information compression, certain situations could escape attention if this were the only available way the executive had to peruse this set of financial data.

Let us imagine that while the "Research and Development" department of the "Commercial Division" is running significantly over budget in "Recruiting Fees", the "Marketing" department of another division is running well under its budget on the same line item. The values for this line item at the company level may then be within the triggers set by the executive, and therefore escape attention on the top screen. This is a case where the problems that may be brewing

Standard Diversified, Ltd.
Recruiting Fees

	Budget YTD	Actual YTD	Variance	% Variance
Commercial Division	445,000	515,000	70,000	15.74
Residential Division	200,000	225,000	25,000	12.50
Government Division	100,000	90,000	-10,000	-10.00

. . .

Figure 33: Sample second menu

Standard Diversified, Ltd.
Recruiting Fees: Commercial Division

	Budget YTD	Actual YTD	Variance	% Variance
Administration	25,000	20,000	-5,000	-20.00
Research	300,000	375,000	75,000	25.00
Manufacturing	10,000	10,000	0	0
Marketing	50,000	60,000	10,000	20.00
Sales	60,000	50,000	10,000	-16.66
. . .				

Figure 34: Sample third menu

within the company offset each other and could fail to come to the forefront when early detection of both problems is critical.

The converse technique of exception-reporting can ensure that these problems surface in an EIS. An EIS application can have an additional functionality that displays screens of exceptions of all line items, irrespective of their level in the structure. The executive then has the option of starting from a screen that displays a list of all exceptions to the triggers at all levels of data consolidation. This report might display a list showing all line items where exceptions occur, starting with company level, then division, then department. In the case we are examining, the "Recruiting Fees" account would not be present at the company level since at this level the values fall within the triggers, but it would show up at the department level in red for "Commercial Division: Research and Development" and in green for "Residential Division: Marketing," shown in Figure 35.

Pointing at any of these line item names would then display the same report of the details of these accounts that could have been reached via drill-down.

Figure 36 summarizes the major differences between executives and operational managers in terms of their work patterns and needs.

PROTOTYPING AS A DESIGN AND DEVELOPMENT METHODOLOGY

The design and development of an EIS cannot often be accommodated using the conventional design methodologies employed for building operational-level systems. Perhaps the major reason that these techniques do not work is the nature of the executive's work itself. Executives are primarily consumers of data, in contrast to operational-level managers and staff, who are generators of data, product, and services.

The conventional systems development process involves a needs assessment, leading to a requirements definition, a functional specification, and finally a systems design and its implementation. When the end user is an operational-level manager, his or her tasks are, in comparison to an executive user's, more product- or service-oriented and usually better defined. The goals of the operational system can therefore be more clearly stated and are more easily developed. From

Standard Diversified Exception Report

	Budget YTD	Actual YTD	Variance	% Variance
Commercial Division:				
Research:				
Recruiting Fees	300,000	375,000	75,000	25.00
Residential Division:				
Marketing:				
Recruiting Fees	200,000	100,000	-100,000	-50.00

Figure 35: Sample exception menu

Executives	Operational Managers
Primarily data consumers	Primarily data generators
Unpredictable data needs	Definable data needs
Infrequent or sporadic usage	Frequent, sustained usage
Need for information compression	Need for data analysis capabilities

Figure 36: Differences in needs of executives and operational managers

such goals, it is straightforward to generate a requirements definition against which the subsequent systems design can be evaluated. The goals of these systems are bounded, and one can determine what outputs are required to meet them. From the output requirements, the necessary input data can be determined.

When the end user is an executive, the goals are much more elusive. The tasks of an executive are generally not product- or service-oriented, and the needed outputs will depend on both the short-range issues at any given point in time and the longer range goals of the organizations. Short- and long-term goals are affected by both internal and external factors. The external influences can come from many sources: the economy, the market, competitors, regulations, the environment, politics, and so on. Most are not directly within the control or influence of the executive, but monitoring status and forecasts of such factors may lead to more timely reactions for defining organizational direction and opportunities.

The unboundedness of these data requirements, both internal and external, leads to frustration on the part of both the end user and the developer when traditional design methodologies are employed. The developer cannot realistically expect the executive to define output requirements in the traditional sense. Conversely, the developer does not feel comfortable designing a system whose goals and outputs have not been defined.

If conventional methods of systems definition and design cannot be used for EIS development, what alternatives are available? One method that has proven successful is prototyping—an iterative process of refinement in both functionality and scope. Many of the design techniques described in the earlier chapters on top-down approaches, structured design, stepwise refinement, use of dummy stubs, and so on, can be applied to prototyping.

Prototyping as a design approach may require some changes in attitude and perspective on the part of the developers. Each review stage can lead to suggestions for changes, requests for more capabilities, and rejections of current approaches. A constantly moving target can prove frustrating to those who resist change or cannot see that progress is being made.

The prototyping technique is most effective if an adequate development environment exists to facilitate a prototyping approach. Traditional programming tools are much too cumbersome to support prototyping, which requires higher-level, less detailed, and less procedurally oriented software tools to be effective. Software that is specifically designed for EIS applications and functionality is increasingly available. As the EIS software market matures, there will be an increase in the availability of off-the-shelf EIS solution packages, in addition to EIS application development tools.

For an EIS application, the prototype should particularly illustrate the "look and feel" of the user interface, including the navigation paths. A good user interface is critical to the success of an EIS application and there is simply no way to know if it works well for the end users until they give it a try. Is it easy to follow a path through the system? Is it clear where you are at any point? Is it clear how to proceed to a lower level or return to a higher level?

In addition, the prototype should illustrate the degree and value of information compression and filtering performed by the system. Provided the software tools permit the building of menus, graphs, and data bases easily, these tools can be used to build and refine such prototypes quickly. It is not necessary to worry at this stage about where all the data will come from when the system is in a production mode. The prototype can be built using either mock data or a small subset of live data. Live data, however small the subset, will usually prove more interesting to the end user. The subset can be defined small enough that, for purposes of the prototype demonstration system, the data can simply be entered manually to build a small data base. For example, assume you are prototyping the EIS budget monitoring system described in the last section. The live data could be entered for five or so line items, such as travel expense, recruiting expense, salary, medical insurance, and life insurance, and could be limited to a couple of departments in each of two divisions of the company. The required data would be the budget figures for the current fiscal year and the actual figures for the first six months. This would amount to 240 numbers for budget and 120 numbers for actual: for budget, 12 (for the number of months) times 5 (for the number of line items) times 4 (for 2 departments in each of 2 divisions); for actual, half of each of the budget figures, representing the first six months only. These figures would be readily available from existing hard-copy financial reports.

The prototype should concentrate on the design of screens that display the data at the company, division, and department level and that illustrate the drill-down facility of the user interface. The prototype can also show the design of the graphic displays and demonstrate how the end user requests these displays and what information is contained on the charts. The exception-reporting mechanism can also be illustrated and the end user allowed to experiment with changing the trigger settings to expand and narrow the number of items listed on the exception report.

The value of the prototype is that the executive is viewing a working system rather than a written description of a design. The "look and feel" of the user interface can be realistically evaluated, and improvements and refinements can be suggested and discussed.

Work on the visual. It's more effective than anything else. People draw conclusions . . . on the basis of what they see . . .

—Robert Ludlum,
The Bourne Supremacy

The interfaces to other systems may be shown on the screens even if the functionality has not yet been developed. For example, print and mail buttons for electronic mail may appear on the screens during the prototype stage but not yet be activated.

The executive can also react to the data content and its presentation. Would additional data be helpful? Should any of the data be eliminated? Would a different report format or graphics provide more useful information?

The developer should respond to the feedback from each prototype review as quickly as possible. The flexibility and power of software tools employed in building the prototype will be a critical factor in determining whether the developer can be as responsive to modifications as a successful prototyping approach demands.

If the tool used to build the prototype is not suitable as the tool to build the eventual full-scale working system, then its utility will be primarily limited to design rather than development. There is also the danger that some of the functionality or presentation modes available within the prototyping tool will not be available in the real development tool and vice versa. Since the full-scale EIS systems will require the same kind of quick response to changing needs and company redirections as the prototype required, the development tool will need to be just as flexible; therefore, the same tool should be used for both. The developers will save time because the software will not have to be redeveloped from scratch when the prototype expands to a full-scale system.

The development tool has additional requirements beyond those of a prototyping tool. It should be able to support increasing numbers of users. It should also support the spread of an EIS to additional application areas, and larger data bases, than may be required during the prototyping stage. An appropriate development tool should accommodate all stages of EIS design and ongoing development.

The expansion of the prototype to a working system can be an evolutionary process. As parts of the interface are deemed suitable for executive needs, these can be more fully developed while other areas are still undergoing refinements. As the data contents are stabilized, development of data feeder systems can commence. When enough data and functionality exists to make the system useful, the prototype can be made available to selected end users while other functionality and data feeder systems are still under development.

The constant feedback and review inherent in the prototyping process has other, less obvious, benefits. The understanding that the developer gains of executive needs and work styles is continually increasing. The executives gain confidence in the abilities of the developers as each presentation is more suited to their needs, having been returned for their review in a timely manner. The interactive process contributes to the building of positive relationships and understanding between end users and developers.

DATA REQUIREMENTS

Defining the data to be included in an EIS is the most difficult area of EIS design. An earlier section discussed the seemingly unbounded and unpredictable nature of an executive's data needs, and the politics that often surround obtaining timely access to the data. There may also be problems of data consistency and comparability. These issues are most likely to make or break the EIS. They are also the ones for which technology provides the least assistance.

Before knowing whether there will be problems gaining access to the data, and whether the data will be comparable once accessible, the data requirements must be identified. While you will want to have technologies that permit the expansion and growth of a successful EIS to something even larger, more comprehensive, and of more value, the initial effort should be a small, well-defined application. "Keep It Simple" applies here as much as it does to operational-level systems.

The choice of an initial application may be evident if your organization has a pressing business problem. It should be one that requires a somewhat sustained effort over several months to solve. A problem with too short a time span may be resolved one way or another before a system can be developed with the appropriate and timely data feeds.

If your organization does not have any business problems, it may not need an EIS. Perhaps your operational systems are providing sufficient information and your corporate communications and management systems are operating so smoothly that both short- and long-term goals are being met. Perhaps, also, your business is such that external conditions and competitors offer no present or future threat to your continued success. All this being true, your company would probably perceive very little, if any, value from pursuing the development of an EIS. However, if you can identify a problem area or an important goal whose progress should be tracked and monitored at an executive or senior level, then you may have the basis for an initial EIS application.

Financial Reporting is frequently chosen as an initial application area.

Finance: The art or science of managing revenues and resources for the best advantage of the manager. The pronunciation of this word with the i long and the accent on the first syllable is one of America's most precious discoveries and possessions.
—Ambrose Bierce
The Devil's Dictionary

Too often, the design of an EIS amounts to little more than "Let's give the executives access to the current printed reports on a terminal." Such a system may provide some small incremental value over an existing paper-based system, especially if it includes some information compression and more random access navigation paths. However, it will not likely be viewed as having enough added value to justify the effort involved and to overcome some of the political objections and obstacles that may be encountered along the way. Monitoring of the financial data will almost always be included as an application in an EIS, but it should be thought of more as a foundation support system than as the main focus.

In a competitive business, external data on the competitors' costs, revenues, and market share shown in comparison with internal data may be a more appropriate focus for an EIS application. Augmenting this data with external news covering product announcements and political, economic, and industry developments may provide new insights into the causes and patterns often buried in internal financial reports. The ability to combine internal, external, quantitative, and qualitative data in new ways may be the real benefit of an EIS.

While technology may not provide a lot of help in coping with the internal data problems of ownership and consistency across organizational lines, it can have a significant impact on obtaining external data. A plethora of electronic data bases now exists and is expanding rapidly. In addition to those providing general services such as news, financial data from publicly traded companies, and stock prices, a growing number of specialized industry data bases are becoming available, via dial-up, floppy disk services, and, more recently, CD Roms. Industry estimates indicate that on-line data base services constitute a $3 billion industry that is growing at the rate of almost 30 percent annually. Approximately 90 percent of the Fortune 500 companies already have some access to these services.

Another approach to adding value to the foundation support systems of financial reporting is to look beyond the simple goals of keeping costs down and revenues up. Systems can be designed to provide higher-level summaries and analyses of cost and revenue components. Costs may be affected by adverse factors such as employee turnover, quality control problems, raw materials markets, inventory levels, and vendor competitiveness. Revenues may be affected by marketing programs, customer satisfaction, consumer trends, sales incentives, and so on. Your company may have already identified some of these areas as problems and set some specific corporate-wide goals to correct them. Focusing an EIS application on specific goals; providing both qualitative and quantitative data from internal and external sources; presenting the data in new formats; and providing easy, efficient accessibility to data and reports may be a powerful addition to a financial monitoring application.

Pertinent data may already be available from a variety of sources within the corporation, but the EIS may become the place where it all comes together and can be viewed from a corporate perspective. While you may not be able to attack the measurement of all corporate goals, and you may not find the necessary data to measure all the components completely, you likely will be able to provide a better tracking system than previously existed and one that requires less, rather than more, of the executive's time.

The measure of success of an EIS is not how often or for how long the executives use it, but whether they are more informed on critical issues than previously and expending less of their time to achieve the same level of understanding. The demands on executives' resources are such that they cannot focus a lot of time on a single task. An EIS should reduce the total time required to monitor the status of the organization, while at the same time increasing the executives' understanding of problems, causes, and effects.

Information needs will vary depending on the overall management style of the company. For example, financially controlled companies may require up-to-date, detailed financial results and have little interest in external information. Strategically controlled companies may require summary-level external information along with bottom-line summaries of financial results and forecasts. Strategically managed companies may prefer detailed external and operational information in conjunction with bottom-line summaries of financial information.

An EIS will be most successful if it supports the needs of the management style most valued within the company. You should select the appropriate level of detail to supply from the broad categories of financial, operational, and external data.

An executive may also have different purposes in mind for each category of information. When the purpose is control, exception-reporting will be a necessary component. When the purpose is to gain intelligence about the industry, external data sources will be required.

The success of an EIS will also depend on the degree to which the executives' work style, management values, and purposes have been considered in the design. The value of the EIS will also depend on the choices of applications that are directly linked to business objectives and problems.

FOCUS ON BUSINESS OBJECTIVES AND PROBLEMS

For reasons discussed earlier in this book, keep the scope of the initial application simple. Select an area that will be viewed as valuable by the target set of end users. Begin with an application that presents status and measurements that pertain to a specific business problem, current year goals and objectives, or critical success factors. Then design outputs to present these measures in a meaningful way to senior management. Finally, build a demo through prototyping to generate interest and elicit feedback from targeted end users; refine and expand the demo into a working system by communicating closely with the operating sponsor.

The areas from which to select EIS applications may be illustrated by the pyramid in Figure 37. The number of issues involved in, and the data required for an EIS, increase as we go further down the pyramid. The approximate duration of the focus on particular issues in each category also increases in the downward direction, as shown in parentheses. Two other scales are indicated on the diagram. To the left is a scale representing the likely executive response to an EIS that measures performance within the selected area, and to the right is a scale representing the difficulty of designing and building an EIS application in the selected area.

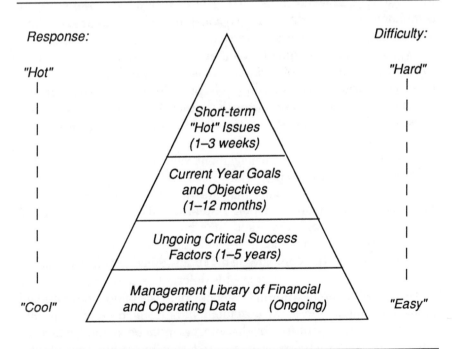

Figure 37: Selection of EIS application areas

The short-term "Hot" issues are most likely to excite the executive, but their short duration makes them less suitable as a focus of an EIS. Unless the required data is already present within the EIS data base, the issues will have changed, and perhaps have been resolved, by the time a system can be put in place. The current year goals and objectives will have high value to the executive and the duration is long enough to put an EIS application in operation.

As you move down the pyramid, the value to the executive diminishes, but the systems become easier to build and the data more readily available. The "management library," at the lowest level of the pyramid, will provide a foundation supporting system for the more focused and exciting applications that are selected from the "hotter" areas.

A well-accepted management theory, "That which is measured improves," applies to the selection of measures for an EIS application. The measurements should relate to the tasks performed by the target users. Abstract objectives such as "Increasing stockholders return on investment" may need to be further broken down into the relevant component parts for different divisional and functional areas within an organization. Many disparate factors may affect return on investment, such as product quality, employee turnover, absenteeism, and so forth. Measurement of these factors may not only be more relevant to specific target end users, but may provide much earlier warning systems for problems other than those that measure bottom-line effects that may occur many months after the contributing causes.

SYSTEM EXPANSION

Successful Executive Information Systems are likely to expand in two directions: new applications and new end users. Often an EIS is adopted first at the corporate level and then expanded to the various division levels of the company. The applications and data bases required at these new levels may be different, necessitating further expansion of the applications set. The work styles of operational-level management may differ in substantial ways from those of corporate executives. The operating-level managers may be more facile with computers, and therefore may request that more functionality be made directly available to the end user than was present in the initial applications. The strengths and weaknesses of the software and hardware systems on which the EIS is based will become increasingly important as the EIS expands. A powerful hardware and software platform, which may have been overkill initially, can begin to pay off in this expansion stage.

The future expansion of an EIS can be made easier or more difficult depending on the initial approach and objectives. If the initial EIS is designed and built to accommodate an individual executive and therefore focuses primarily on his or her specific needs, work style, and "hot issues," the system may not be sufficiently generalized to serve other end users. And what happens to the EIS if this particular end user is reassigned or leaves the company? On the other hand, an EIS that is designed and built to serve corporate needs and facilitate management communication and effectiveness among groups is less likely to be thrown out after a management reorganization, and is more likely to be useful and expand to other groups and levels within the company. Access to an EIS should be distributed to the operating management and staff personnel within an organization who can use the information and capabilities to help achieve the goals and objectives it measures. Its usage should not be limited to the most senior executives.

Expanding the number of users may create problems in several areas. On mainframe-based systems, response time may deteriorate as the number of users increases. On stand-alone, PC-based systems, maintenance time will increase linearly with the number of users because each individual workstation will need to be updated. Cost per user is another factor to consider. Mainframe-based systems will often achieve a lower cost per user as the system expands, while PC-based systems will retain the same cost per user as the number of

---

Future: That period of time in which our affairs prosper, our friends are true and our happiness is assured.
—Ambrose Bierce,
The Devil's Dictionary

---

users increases. However, PC-based system costs may increase as the number of applications, and hence the local disk capacity, increases. The future size and scope of an EIS deserve careful thought when choosing the initial approaches.

A widely distributed EIS can benefit both the individual and the corporation. The EIS can put individuals in closer contact with more key staff so all can share a common and more informed view of the company. It may also reduce unnecessary layers of reporting requirements and staff. The EIS can serve as a catalyst for change by refocusing the attention of the organization on new goals and objectives, and by providing a more effective mechanism for communicating and tracking progress toward them.

SUMMARY

This summary is organized by chapter and shows the major questions and topics covered in each.

1. **What is the user's role?**

   Clearly specify *what* the system must do by separating the problem definition phase from the problem solution phase.

   Establish clear relationships between external needs and system requirements as a basis for impact analysis of subsequent design decisions and cost-benefit tradeoffs.

   Use your area-content expertise to provide project leadership, direction, and feedback during the development process.

2. **How is the scope of the system determined?**

   Assess external needs; establish system goals and measurable objectives.

   Limit the initial system scope to well-defined functions with identifiable benefits to be derived from automation.

   Analyze the external information requirements of each function and define these requirements in terms of data items.

3. **Can development costs be controlled?**

   Plan to build the system in small increments.

   Avoid needless complexity.

   Choose design solutions that best suit the problem.

   Be aware of the cost implications of various design alternatives and capabilities.

4. **How can users do their own system analysis?**

   Develop an overall analysis plan in which each step builds upon the last one.

   Make use of top-down problem-solving techniques that simplify problem analysis.

5. **What are the steps involved in producing a requirements definition?**

   Define information needs.

   Determine required inputs.

   Define data relationships.

   Define computer outputs.

   Define inquiry capabilities.

   Identify sources of inputs.

   Define data-entry procedures.

   Specify data validation requirements.

   Define data protection requirements.

   Specify data derivation rules.

6. **What is the user's role after requirements are specified?**

   Review design proposals and decide among the alternatives.

   Develop external procedures necessary for system operation.

   Develop acceptance testing procedures and evaluation criteria.

   Evaluate system performance and end results.

   Specify required adjustments, refinements, and corrections.

7. **How can the user control the end results of software development?**

   Choose management strategies that place the user in the decision-making role and develop a sense of ownership in the system on the part of potential end users.

   Choose implementation strategies that:

- provide progress measurements meaningful to the user;
- make user feedback integral to the development process;
- optimize chances for success and minimize risk factors;
- use development resources most productively to achieve system goals.

8. **What other factors affect system utility?**

Develop well-defined goals and audiences for required documentation. Make the production of documentation integral to the development process.

Give a high priority to effective end-user training and allocate resources commensurate with its importance.

Define computer interfaces that are appropriate to the type of task, the type of end user, and the frequency of use.

9. **When requirements change in the future, will the software be usable?**

Identify those areas where change is likely to occur.

Plan automated maintenance systems to handle those changes that must be implemented without programmer intervention.

Incorporate the use of software development tools and methods that minimize the need for reprogramming and that help manage change effectively.

Be aware of the typical evolution path of application requirements within organizations.

Build data bases around organizational subjects to permit orderly future expansion and incremental application integration.

10. **What are the major areas of end-user computing?**

Office automation, decision support, and executive information.

11. **What are the major considerations affecting the choice of hardware for an EIS?**

Acceptable response times, system capacity, costs, and issues of hardware compatibility.

12. **What are the major considerations affecting the choice of software for an EIS?**

    Fast prototype development and enhancement ability, centrally controlled maintenance capability, easy-to-use interface, and acceptable response times.

13. **Why might a separate EIS data base be preferable to direct links to operational data bases?**

    The performance of the operational systems is not disrupted by executives' ad hoc queries and analyses, which are unpredictable.

    The information needed by the executives is not being changed as it is being used. The users have a need for an accurate, defined point-in-time slice of the data.

    Operational data bases are optimized for high-volume updating such as transaction processing and are not necessarily suitable for ad hoc queries by executive end users.

14. **What are the basic functional requirements of an EIS?**

    Data Access:

    > Access to internal and external data
    >
    > Access to historical and forecast data

    Interfaces:

    > Intuitive and easy-to-use interface
    >
    > Links to electronic mail for communications

    Information Compression:

    > Efficient navigation via "drill-down"
    >
    > Highlight problems via "exception-reporting"

    Display Modes:

    > Graphic presentation for trend analysis
    >
    > Combinations of qualitative and quantitative data for context.

BIBLIOGRAPHY

Enger, Norman L. *Management Standards for Developing Information Systems*. New York: AMACOM, 1976.

Date, C.J. *An Introduction to Database Systems*. Reading, Mass.: Addison-Wesley, 1981.

Martin, James. *Computer Data Base Organization*. Englewood Cliffs, N.J.: Prentice-Hall, 1977.

————*Principles of Data-Base Management*. Englewood Cliffs, N.J.: Prentice-Hall, 1976.

Myers, G.J. *Composite/Structured Design*. New York: Van Nostrand Reinhold Co., 1978.

————*Software Reliability: Principles and Practices*. New York: John Wiley and Sons, 1976.

Orr, Kenneth T. *Structured Systems Development*. New York: Yourdon, 1977.

Rockart, John F. and Delong, David W. *Executive Support Systems: The Emergence of Top Management Computer Use*. Dow Jones Irwin, 1988.

Tausworthe, R.C. *Standardized Development of Computer Software*. Englewood Cliffs, N.J.: Prentice-Hall, 1977.

Yourdon, E. and Constantine, L.L. *Structured Design*. New York: Yourdon, 1978.

Yourdon, E. *Managing the Structured Techniques*. New York: Yourdon, 1979.

INDEX

Auerbach, 20

Business planning systems, 124

Committee,
  design, 90
  review, 89
Computer-assisted training, 107
Composite design, 92
Cooperative processing, 142
Course writer, 107

Data
  derivation, 78
  dictionaries, 120
  encryption, 77
  protection, 75
  validation, 74
Datapro, 20
Decision support, 132
Definition, requirements, 58–59
DeLong, David W., 134, 139
Dictionaries, data, 120
Disaster recovery, 76
Distributed processing, 123
Documentation,
  system development, 102
  system maintenance, 103
  system operations, 103
Drill-down, 150
Dummy stubs, 94, 95, 160

Exception-reporting, 150
Executive
  champion, 140
  information systems, 134
  support systems, 134

External system, 27
  tasks, 55

Forms editor, 117

Help, on-line, 106

Independence,
  data, 119
  machine, 118
  program, 116
Information
  center, 133
  compression, 151
Input-Process-Output Model, 25
Interactiveness, 31
Interface system, 29
  tasks, 56
Interface modes
  command, 111
  conversational, 108
  menu, 110
  skeletal screen, 112
Interfaces,
  batch, 33
  on-line, 33
  real-time, 36
Internal system, 37
  tasks, 57

LAN (local area network), 124, 142,
  143

Maintenance, automated, 115, 173
Management information systems, 123
MIT Sloan School of Management, 134

Navigation paths, 149

Office automation, 132
Operating sponsor, 141

Parameter files, 116
PERT charts, 95
Postimplementation report, 85
Project team, 90
Prototyping, 157

Recovery, disaster, 76
Requirements definition, 58–59
Rockart, John F., 134, 139

Structured programming, 92
Subject data bases, 125
Systems,
   automated maintenance, 115, 173

business planning, 124
cooperative processing, 142
distributed processing, 123
executive information, 134
interface, 29
internal, 37
management information, 123

Test,
   acceptance, 83
   integration, 95
   parallel system, 83
Test data bases, 106
Test drivers, 96
Top-down implementation, 92
   conservative, 97
   look-ahead, 98
   radical, 96

K